George Carr

Sermons

Volume 2

George Carr

Sermons
Volume 2

ISBN/EAN: 9783337116835

Printed in Europe, USA, Canada, Australia, Japan

Cover: Foto ©Lupo / pixelio.de

More available books at **www.hansebooks.com**

SERMONS.

BY THE LATE

REV. GEORGE CARR,

SENIOR CLERGYMAN of the ENGLISH EPISCOPAL
CONGREGATION in EDINBURGH.

IN TWO VOLUMES.

VOL. II.

THE SEVENTH EDITION.

To which are prefixed,

AN ELEGANT ENGRAVING, AND SOME ACCOUNT OF THE AUTHOR.

———◆———

EDINBURGH:

PRINTED FOR BELL & BRADFUTE; AND
G. G. J. & J. ROBINSON, AND J. MURRAY, LONDON.

M.DCC.XCI.

CONTENTS.

SERM.   Page

I. *Wisdom of a religious course of life*, - 1
II. *Religious employment of time*, - 17
III. *Error of conforming to fashionable vices*, - - - 30
IV. *On conscience*, - - 44
V. *House of mourning*, - - 59
VI. *Positive institutions inferior to moral duties*, - - - 73
VII. *Goodness of God in the redemption*, 86
VIII. *On resignation to the will of God*, 102
IX. *On the general judgment*, - 117
X. *On public worship*.——Preached at opening the New Episcopal Chapel at Edinburgh, - - 132
XI. *Internal excellence of the Gospel*, 153
XII. *Ascension*, - - 166
XIII. *On Divine Grace and human co-operation*, - - 183
XIV. *Against an improper love of this world*, - - - 200

XV. Sin

CONTENTS.

Serm.	Page
XV. *Sin of profaning* the name of God,	214
XVI. *Duty of doing as we would be done by,*	226
XVII. *Sins of infirmity and presumption,*	242
XVIII. *On the resurrection,*	257
XIX. *On peace,*	272
XX. *On contentment,*	285
XXI. *Duty of exemplary manners,*	298
XXII. *Peace of mind the attendant on virtue,*	311
XXIII. *Methods by which God has revealed his will to mankind,*	325
XXIV. *General instances of God's goodness to men,*	340
XXV. *Men sojourners upon earth.—* Preached on New-year's day,	355
XXVI. *Against evil-speaking,*	369
XXVII. *On vitious habits,*	383

SERMON I.

Wisdom of a religious course of life.

Job xxviii. 28.

Behold, the fear of the Lord, that is wisdom; and to depart from evil, is understanding.

OUR CREATOR, who has appointed this world to be the present scene of our being, has been pleased to place good and evil, life and death, before us, and has left them to our own free election; has intrusted our happiness or misery to our own conduct, and made them to depend upon ourselves. The most important concernment of life, therefore, is, to make a right and prudent choice. It is of the last consequence to consider well, by what principles we shall form our conduct; upon what plan we shall act; whether we shall search for the proper happiness of our nature in the paths of virtue, or in the ways of vice: whether we shall attend to the directions of unerring Wisdom, or follow the counsels of our own passions: whether we shall pursue the moral plan which the light of Nature discovers, and which the light of the Gospel illustrates and enforces; or whether we shall reject the divine instructions, and, regardless of consequences here or hereafter, seize the pleasures of the present hour, walk in the ways of our heart and in the sight of our eyes, and go on wherever seducement may invite, or inclination prompt us.

The wisdom of a religious choice, asserted in the text, may appear from the following considerations.

1. Certain it is, that the whole body of moral or religious laws, are the laws of the wise and good LEGISLATOR of the world,

world, whose design in imparting to us our being, was doubtless to communicate a portion of his happiness; and whose view in giving us laws, was as certainly to promote that happiness, and to improve it to the utmost capacity of our nature. For, most assuredly, he can have no personal interest in view. He can require nothing from us for his own sake, not even the worship we are to render him, nor the glory we are to ascribe to him. Our imperfect praises and ignorant adorations can add nothing to the fulness of his felicity; nor can we detract from it by our neglect or disobedience. For *can a man be profitable to God? or is it gain to him if thou makest thy ways perfect? If thou be righteous, what givest thou him? or what receiveth he at thine hand?*

His perfections also forbid us to suppose that he can derive pleasure from the dependence or servitude of his creatures; or that he can delight in issuing arbitrary injunctions, or despotic mandates. His laws can be considered in no other light than as rule of conduct, resulting from the frame and constitution of our nature, and necessary to our well-being. While Religion, therefore, is our guide, and we conduct our steps by the direction of the supreme LAWGIVER, the divine wisdom is our security that our paths shall terminate in peace.

II. In order to vindicate the wisdom of a religious conduct, it may not be improper to obviate a prejudice too commonly propagated, and too easily received, That the felicities of the next world are not to be obtained, according to the strict terms of Christianity, without renouncing the enjoyments of the present. Religion is too often represented with an unpleasing countenance and severe aspect, interdicting pleasures, exacting hard services, commanding us to wage perpetual war with the world and our own nature. Were this representation just, we could draw no conclusion against the wisdom of religious obedience;—since infinite is the disproportion between the two worlds,—between time

time and eternity; and we could not think it an unreasonable condition of eternal salvation if we were required to employ the whole of a short life in the immediate service of God. An eternity of happiness is surely worth the obedience and service of a few years, how difficult soever the obedience may be.

But the merciful Author of religion has not dealt thus hardly with mankind. Its wise and easy restraints preclude us from no enjoyments that reason approves; from none that we can desire with prudence, or enjoy with safety. Religion prohibits only those specious, but destructive, evils, which the passions of mankind have dressed up in the disguise of pleasure; those irregular pursuits, in which no wise man would ever place his happiness, or could ever find it.

God, who has filled the earth with his goodness, and surrounded us with objects which he made agreeable to our nature, cannot be supposed to require us to reject his bounty, and to look on them all as on the fruit of that tree in paradise, which was pleasant to the eye, but forbidden to be tasted. Too apt, indeed, are we to imitate the disobedience of our first parent; and like him, not satisfied with eating freely of every tree which our CREATOR offers to us in this garden of nature, we too often listen to every tempter, and expect to find pleasure in the forbidden fruits of vice. But be the pleasures of vice what they may, there is still a superior pleasure in subduing the passions of it: for it is the pleasure of reason and wisdom; the pleasure of an intellectual, not a mere animal being; a pleasure that will always stand the test of reflection, and never fails to impart true and permanent satisfaction.

The duties of religion are indeed, in all respects, so conformable to those principles which our CREATOR has impressed on our mind, and strike such harmony upon the soul, and diffuse such complacency through it, that the very argument of pleasure, which forms generally the greatest

greatest prejudice against religion, proves, when rightly understood, the most powerful incitement to it.——Which leads me to observe,

III. That the wisdom of a religious conduct may appear from its being the sure foundation of that peace of mind which is the chief constituent of happiness. The reflection on a life employed in serving GOD, and attending to the proper ends of our being; a consciousness of integrity towards him; and the consequent hopes of an interest in his favour, and of an happy immortality when this short and transitory scene is no more,—will be a never failing source of satisfaction and delight. Hence arise a thousand self-gratulations.

What Solomon observes of wisdom, is equally true of peace of mind: *The merchandise of it is better than the merchandise of silver, and the gain thereof than fine gold. She is more precious than rubies, and all the things thou canst desire are not to be compared to her.* But this is a happiness which vice must ever be a stranger to, and none

but

but the virtuous and good ever can enjoy. Avarice cannot find it in wealth, nor Senfuality in vitious gratifications, nor Ambition in honours and diſtinctions; nor is it to be found but in the reflections of the virtuous mind. The children of this world may succeed in the immediate objects of their purſuit,—honours, power, or wealth; but cannot obtain happineſs, or peace of mind,—the end for which thoſe objects are purſued. This is a reward which the Author of our being confers only on thoſe that obey him, and ſuffers none but the virtuous and religious to poſſeſs.

True it is, that the moſt perfect virtue is not productive of pure, unmixed happineſs. The condition of human life will not permit us to expect a total exemption from evils. Religion will indeed bring with it internal peace of mind, but cannot ſecure us from external contingencies; from fraud, injuſtice, or violence, to which the iniquity of the world will expoſe us; nor from pain, ſorrow, or ſickneſs, to which our

our frame is by nature subject. But tho' these, or other afflictions, may be the lot of the good man; yet his peace of mind will alleviate the weight of those afflictions, and support him under them,—which is next to an exemption from them. Religion will not reverse the distinctions of station which Providence has appointed: it will neither give riches to the poor, nor liberty to the captive; but it will administer consolation to both; it will teach acquiescence and contentment; it will teach, that godliness is the best riches, freedom from sin the most valuable liberty. Religion will not secure us from the passions of others; but it will protect us from our own; it will humanize the mind, and soften it into moderation, and teach all our passions a due subjection to reason and duty.

But further: Religion is not less friendly in its influence on social than private life; and is equally conducive to the happiness of the public, and of individuals. So far, therefore, as every one's happiness is connected

nected with and dependent on that of the public, it becomes his interest, and his wisdom, upon this account, to be religious. It is not in human reason to devise rules better calculated for the security and peace and happiness of social life, than those prescribed by religion. It forbids all fraud, violence, and oppression; corrects all acrimony of temper, all asperity of manners; recommends a just discharge of the duties proper to our respective stations; bids us regard every man as our brother, equally related to GOD with ourselves. It instructs us to be liberal to the wants of others, compassionate to their afflictions; to be easy to be reconciled, ready to forgive them.

All the virtues that can render a people secure and flourishing, all the duties that the best political laws require as necessary or conducive to the public tranquillity, are enjoined by our religion; and all the crimes they forbid, as subversive of public peace and order, are prohibited by it: so that the wisest legislators bear testimony to
the

the wisdom and excellence of religion; which has this peculiar advantage above all human laws, that whereas their restraints can extend only to external behaviour, and bind the hand, religion reaches the heart, regulates its movements, and purifies that source and fountain of action.

And were the practice of religion generally to prevail; if all men would act under the influence of its principles, and be sober, honest, temperate, and industrious; they would escape more than half the evils that afflict mankind. It is easy to see, that the natural consequences of such universal virtue would present to the mind a perfect portrait, a finished image, of public happiness: an image, indeed, which the mind may form to itself, and contemplate;—but which the corruption of mankind, it is to be feared, will never suffer to have more than an ideal, never a real, existence. But in whatever proportion probity, integrity, benevolence, and the rest of the virtues, prevail in any nation; in the same proportion will that nation feel

feel those happy consequences, which, were mens virtue perfect, would be as perfect happiness as the condition of mortality will admit.

Lastly, The wisdom of a religious life may hence appear, because such a conduct is infinitely preferable, infinitely more prudent and secure, when we take futurity into consideration. It is utterly impossible to produce any proof of our non-existence hereafter; and were we capable of conceiving, that the evidence for, or against, the certainty of a future state, is not decisive, and that the arguments on both sides equiponderate; yet it would be prudent, surely, to become adventurers for another world, and provide for the important chance. If there be no future account to be given, no existence after death, but all beyond the grave is a land of silence and darkness, a state of oblivion and insensibility, (the utmost that vice and libertinism can wish); yet, even then, the good man will rest equally with the wicked in that state where all things are alike forgotten;

gotten; and suffers nothing in this life, upon account of his religion, but the want of those pleasures which are not to be purchased but at the expence of his virtue, his peace of mind, and his hopes of immortality; those hopes, which, were they even delusive and visionary, yet are eminently subservient and essential even to our present peace: for these are the best ingredients to sweeten the bitter cup that the world often administers; from these alone can be derived support under adversities, or satisfaction even in enjoyments. If religion should hereafter prove a mistake, it is a mistake for which we shall not be accountable. Should our hopes prove fallacious, and our faith be all error and delusion, we cannot be more unhappy than the wicked, when both are to be no more. But, if our faith and hopes be well-grounded (and we have most certainly sufficient evidence of their truth), the righteous are then for ever inconceivably blessed.

On the other hand, it is not in the power of the wicked man to extinguish in
him-

himself all ideas of GOD the Judge of the world, and all apprehensions of a future existence. And when he considers it only as possible, that, this life ended, he may enter into another more important state of being, for which he has made no provision; that there may be a day of judgment, there may be a future tribunal, where he must appear, and where he can make no defence; this, this alone will be sufficient to draw a black, melancholy veil over all his enjoyments, and open a prospect full of horror. It is virtue alone that can look forward into futurity with any degree of confidence or satisfaction. Vice is no competitor there, nor ever thinks of laying claim to future rewards: on the contrary, the wicked man must be often alarmed with fears and apprehensions, that, as he is by nature accountable, an account must one day be given; and that, as punishment is due, punishment may overtake him hereafter.

Upon the whole, the good man enjoys, generally, superior happiness in this world; and,

and, in the next, stands alone, without any rival, in his hopes and pretensions. Be it then our care to order our steps so, that, without turning aside to the right hand or to the left, we may persevere in that line of wisdom to which the wise and good Author of our being has directed us; and live ever obedient to HIM, whose precepts are favours, whose restrictions are mercies, whose laws are the laws of kindness;—not mere dictates of will, not the arbitrary mandates of power,—but rules of conduct, resulting from our nature, and essential to our well-being.

The divine laws are the instructions of our CREATOR, the counsels of our Supreme PARENT, pointing out to us the way to felicity. Let us then believe, that he has, with parental care, consulted our interests in all his instructions; and let us show our piety and prudence in our obedience to them. *O how I love thy law!* says the Psalmist, convinced of its supreme excellence: *it is my meditation all the day. Thou, through thy commandments, hast made me wiser*

wiser than mine enemies; for they are ever with me. I have more understanding than my teachers; for thy testimonies are my meditation. I am wiser than the aged, because I keep thy commandments. Impressed with the same conviction as the Psalmist, let each of us adopt his language, and concur in the piety of his resolutions: *Teach me, O Lord, the way of thy statutes, and so shall I keep it unto the end. Give me understanding, and I will keep thy law; yea, I will keep it with my whole heart. I will meditate on thy precepts, and have respect unto thy ways; I will delight myself in thy statutes; I will not forget thy word.*

SER-

SERMON II.

Religious employment of Time.

EPHES. v. 15. 16.

See then that ye walk circumspectly, not as fools, but as wife, redeeming the time.

THIS admonition of the apostle is well worthy of the consideration of mankind in general, as well as of those to whom it was particularly addressed. For mankind in general, far from the circumspection required by the apostle, are but too guilty of indifference and inadvertence to religious duties. Religion they are too apt to consider as a matter of slight and easy concern, and to pass away life in the indolence of security, and in an inattention which they would think highly criminal where any other interest than that of eternity was at stake. The present opportunities of ensuring our salvation we suffer to pass unregarded by us. Of nothing are we more wasteful than of time; than which, nothing is more valuable. We are always ready to part with it upon cheap and easy terms, and to give what we can spare from wordly concerns to every one that asketh. Little of our time, it is to be feared, will turn to account with regard to our future interest: much of it is doubtless unprofitably, too much perhaps criminally, wasted; in which case, both our time and ourselves are lost for ever.

Should we sit down, and take an account of our years, and calculate the expence of our time, and mark its various articles, how little would generally appear, at the foot of the account, expended in the true ends of living, or employed in such purposes as will be of use in the life to come!

The precept in the text, which directs us to walk circumspectly, and to redeem our time, implies attention in employing the present opportunities of life; and care in correcting the errors of the past.

In this discourse, then, I shall consider, 1*st*, How attentive we ought to be to employ our present time in the duties of Religion; and, 2*dly*, Shall offer some admonitions, to assist in correcting the errors of our former conduct.

I. Let us observe how attentive we ought to be to employ our present time in the duties of Religion. The importance of this work calls for all the attention we can give it. For what can we conceive of higher importance than the salvation of the Soul? This is the one thing, above all other things, needful; in comparison of which, honours, power, pleasures, possessions, every thing that the world has to offer, is of no moment or value. If, then, the salvation of our souls demands our care; if to attain the favour of Heaven, and an immortality of happiness, be of importance; if thefe are objects highly confequential to us, the duties of religion, which are neceffary to that end, are of equal confequence, and equally demand our attention.

But important and neceffary as our attention to the duties of religion muft appear—the neceffity of this attention will be ftill more apparent, when we confider the extent and difficulty of the work we have to perform. For it is not fo eafy a tafk as fome may apprehend, faithfully to difcharge the duties which religion requires, and to walk in all the commandments of God blamelefs: no eafy tafk rightly to conduct and difcipline our paffions; to correct the various diforders, and wrong propenfities, of our nature; to turn the bias of our inclinations from evil to good; to guard our hearts from evil thoughts, and to reftrain the tongue from uncharitable cenfure; to have a mind equal to every condition; in adverfity to be patient and refigned, in profperity to be humble and humane, under provocations to be

meek

meek and benevolent: to possess our soul with a due reverence of our MAKER; to keep the will in a perfect submission to the will of Heaven; to set GOD always before us; to have our duty always in our eye; to keep the soul always awake to its supreme and immortal interests; to oppose the stream of criminal custom and fashion; to preserve an unspotted purity amidst the pollutions of the world; not to be tempted by the example or persuasion, the friendship or reproaches, of others; and in general, to restrain all our inclinations and passions, our desires and aversions, within the bounds of duty, to order our steps steadily in the paths of religion, to improve to the best advantage every talent intrusted to our care, and to prepare ourselves to be fit inhabitants of that holy place where nothing impure can enter.

And as the task is arduous and important, so the time to perform it is but short. How inconsiderable is the natural term of human life, even in its utmost extent! and how is this scanty measure of our years still farther abridged by various causes!

Part of life passes away before the dawn of reason gives us a discernment of good and evil, and a great part of it is elapsed before we arrive at any maturity of understanding. If to this we add the infirmities and disorders that usually attend and cloud the evening of life, how short then is the intermediate day for the moral culture of the soul? Especially when we further reflect, that the demands of our respective stations, and the unavoidable cares of the world, consume a large portion of it. And if to these necessary deductions we add the casual ones that we must all inevitably meet with, it will appear what a small part of our abode here we have to bestow on the moral improvement of the mind, the care of the soul, or the concernments of a future existence.

If thus contracted, then, is the whole term allotted us for gaining or losing an happy immortality; if business of such importance is to be transacted and executed in so short a space;—what attention, what circumspection, what good husbandry,

dry, must be requisite to the prudent employment of it? This consideration of the shortness of our time, should be a powerful inducement to apply, without delay, to the great work and business of life, and dispatch it with becoming diligence; lest, by neglecting or deferring it, our lives may draw to an end before the great work of life be finished, perhaps indeed before it is begun, and we may be hurried out of this world before we have made provision for the next.

Of high concern, therefore, it is, not to spend our hours in vanity, not to suffer our time to pass without improvement; not to live a day in vain; not to defer till to-morrow or to any supposed hereafter, the duty that ought to be done at present. For this supposed hereafter may perhaps never be in our possession. We know not whether to-morrow may be ours: for, short as Nature has made our term of life, it is often rendered still shorter by various unforeseen and unavoidable contingencies. Exposed always to a thousand accidents, we know not what a day, or an hour, may bring forth. Life is held by fo uncertain a tenure, that in the midſt of it we are ſaid to be in death. No time but the preſent, therefore, we can confider as our own. The time that is paſt was ours indeed; and as we employed it well or ill, will accordingly be placed to our account. The time that is future, we cannot reckon upon; it may, or may not, be ours. We are fecure of nothing but the prefent: and no portion of time beyond the prefent may poſſibly be granted us. The prefent time, therefore, we ſhould feize, and improve to the beſt purpoſes; and make that our own, by virtue and wiſdom, which, when once paſt, can never be recalled. If we loſe the preſent, we loſe all that is, all that perhaps ever may be, ours. It is the immediate buſineſs of to-day, to ferve GOD, and to be uſeful and do good to our fellow-creatures. Let us not then poſtpone till to-morrow the immediate and proper buſineſs and duty of to-day.

Having thus confidered how attentive
we

we ought to be to employ the prefent time in the duties of religion, I fhall proceed,

II. To offer fome admonitions to affift us in redeeming the time that is paft.

Time is indeed, ftrictly fpeaking, irrecoverable; the hours that are fled cannot be recalled; and time, in a literal fenfe, cannot be regained or redeemed. but in a moral fenfe it may,—by carefully recollecting the conduct of former years; reviewing the volume of our paft life, perufing with an attentive eye its various paffages, and correcting and amending its numerous errors. To this end a careful retrofpect is requifite, in order to obferve in what manner we have performed the duties we owe to GOD and our fellow-creatures; whether there be any fin which we have not duly repented of, and for which we have not implored the divine forgivenefs; whether there be any injury done to our neighbour, for which we have not made fufficient reparation; whether our gratitude to the Divine BEING has been fuited to the bleffings we have received

ved from him; and whether the good or kind offices we have done to others, were proportioned to our ability of doing them. We should observe in what duties we have been most defective; what temptations have generally prevailed, what virtues have been weakest, what passions most irregular. By thus inquiring into the disorders of the soul, we shall be best able to apply proper remedies, and rectify whatever we find amiss.

It might be particularly useful to look back on our transgressions, and the seducements by which we were tempted. If, in compliance with temptation, we have at any time forgotten what we owe to GOD, and have departed from our duty, let us recollect what degree of happiness we acquired by such transgressions, and what compensation they have made us for the loss of our integrity, for the loss, perhaps, of our peace of mind, and for the loss of the approbation and countenance of Heaven. Was interest the temptation? let us make a fair estimate of our profit, and

compute

compute how much satisfaction we have received from dishonest gain; from adding house to house, or field to field. Has it made any addition to our peace of mind? has it not rather been the perpetual occasion of painful recollections; and is there not, upon the whole, a large balance of misery against us? Or was pleasure the seducement? Was it not fallacious? Did it not fall far short of what our hopes had promised? And what of it now remains, but the regret of having pursued it, and the bitter remembrance of its guilt? If we thus reflect upon the unhappy consequences of former transgressions, we shall be less inclined to yield to future temptations, knowing that they terminate in sorrow and remorse. And thus we may be said to redeem the past time, by reviewing and correcting the errors of our former conduct, and repairing the damages we have received from it.

Let us then seriously consider, that the future state and condition of our being for eternal ages depends upon our present con-

conduct and behaviour; and that the prize of immortal happiness is not to be obtained, but by a religious employment of the short and uncertain term of years allotted us in this life. How vigilant and careful, then, ought we to be to provide for the great end of our being, the salvation of our souls, by a wise employment of the present time, and by retrieving the miscarriages of the past!

But here I would observe, that to the religious employment of our time, it is not necessary that it should be all devoted to the more immediate duties of religion. It is not necessary that we should be always on our knees, or have always our eyes or hearts elevated towards heaven. This our condition in the world will not admit. But we employ our time well, when we divide it between the concerns of this life and those of the next; when we attend to the duties of our respective stations and employments, and in our intercourse with the world act always with justice, uprightness, and integrity; when we decline all opportunities of returning ill offices, and lay hold on every occasion of doing a kind one; when we let temperance govern our appetites, and meekness moderate our paſſions; when we begin and cloſe the day with adoring our CREATOR, who made both it and us,—and with intreating his forgiveneſs, protection, and aſſiſtance; and, on days ſet apart for the ſolemn worſhip of the ALMIGHTY, when we make his more immediate ſervice our employment, and retire from all other cares to that which is moſt needful, the care of our ſouls. This is to employ our time religiouſly: and, by thus employing it, we ſhall avoid that compunction and regret which the dying ſinner feels, when he looks back on the years he has waſted in folly, and wiſhes in vain to recal the hours that are fled; we ſhall neither neglect the concerns of this world, nor thoſe of the next; we ſhall perform the duties required from us here, and ſhall prepare our ſouls for that immortal ſtate of felicity into which we hope finally to enter.

SERMON III.

Error of conforming to fashionable Vices.

ROM. xii. 2.

Be not conformed to this world.

THE corruption and degeneracy of human nature has been the common and just subject of virtuous complaint in every age. And the scripture, conformably to the general sentiments of mankind, represents the world as in a state of depravation, degenerated from its original purity,—as a corrupt and corrupting scene, where all our attention and vigilance

lance will be required to guard against the contagion of its vices, and where persuasions and examples will be always soliciting our compliance with prevailing manners.

Amidst these dangers, and this prevalence of vice, it may be proper to attend to the fatal consequences of conforming to the corrupt manners and vices of the world.

I. When virtue is neglected,—disregarded by the many, and discountenanced by the great; when the public manners are corrupt, and vice has the authority of numbers on its side; we are often weak enough to comply with the seducements of example, and to fall in with the common degeneracy. We cannot but observe how powerful and universal is the influence and authority of fashion, or popular example; with what passive submission we obey its guidance; how soon we become voluntary slaves, and resign our manners, our sentiments, and modes of living, to its dominion. Even our religious

gious opinions, and our moral deportment, we are apt to form, as we do our language, by imitation; and pay a more prompt obedience to the dictates of fashion, custom, and example, than to the laws of reason, conscience, and duty: and often act as if we had no reason, judgement, or conscience, to be our guide; but were implicitly led, and as it were mechanically impelled and directed, by the sentiments and manners of the world. With a great part of mankind, with the vulgar at least of every rank, fashion and example should seem to supply the place of reason and reflection.

But powerful as the influence of public manners may be, it cannot vindicate or excuse criminal compliances. For right and wrong, moral good and evil, are founded, not on the capricious rules of fashion or custom, not on the fluctuating opinions of the world, not on the variable institutions of human appointment; but have a certain, permanent, invariable, establishment in Nature. Our
CREATOR,

CREATOR, when he gave us our being, gave us an immutable law for our conduct, from which no opinions or customs, no power, can authorise us to depart. Sooner shall heaven and earth pass away, than the least part of that law be antiquated or repealed.

This law our CREATOR has revealed to us by the light of nature, and has inscribed it upon the heart. He has taught us, by our moral feelings, by the dictates of reason, as well as by the precepts of revelation, our duties to him, to our fellow-creatures, and to ourselves; duties so clearly revealed, that whenever we reflect on our conduct, such reflection is invariably attended with a sense and consciousness of the rectitude or iniquity of our actions, and of their disagreement or conformity to the law of reason. The law of reason is the primary, the eternal, and immutable law of morality; it is the law of every intellectual being; it is the law of man, and it is the law of GOD; a law which he himself ever invariably observes, and the violation of which he must ever disapprove in his creatures. And this law comes further recommended and enforced by the law of revelation.

If, then, this law has a firm and immoveable foundation in nature, and in the gospel; if our obligation, consequently, to moral duties, be indispensable and immutable; how evident an error is it to pay more regard to the manners and example of the world, than to the monitions of reason and conscience! What an indignity to the SOVEREIGN of the universe, to forsake his eternal laws of righteousness, prescribed by unerring wisdom, in order to comply with human corruptions and fashionable modes of vice! Let us not presume, that the JUDGE of all the earth will grant an indulgence to any species of sin, merely because it is general and prevailing; or that the multitude of offenders will screen any individual from the inflictions of justice. For our SAVIOUR has informed us, that *wide is the gate, and broad the way, that leads to destruction, and that*

that many there be which go in thereat; and that strait is the gate, and narrow the way, that leadeth unto life, and that few there be that find it.

When GOD saw that the wickedness of man was great, and that all flesh had corrupted his way upon earth, he sent, we know, a general deluge to exterminate the inhabitants of the earth, and to transmit to future generations a lasting and awful memorial of his justice and resentment against sin, however universal and prevailing. In human governments, indeed, particular criminals may escape, and multitudes may be pardoned for the sake of expediency; but such a conduct can have no place under the divine administration. The perfections of the Divine Nature render it equally impossible that any transgressor should escape his eye, or that any inconvenience should ensue from the punishment of multitudes. If the whole world were by his sentence at once doomed to immediate annihilation, and the whole human race extirpated, he can call other worlds, worlds without number, into being.

The consequences of sin must therefore prove inevitably fatal to the sinner, in this life, or a future. For if there be a GOD who superintends and governs the world, and who made us moral and accountable beings, it must be a proper act of his government to bring every individual to judgment. The rectitude of the Divine Nature will manifest his approbation of virtue and his aversion to sin, by rendering to every man according to his deeds, and regulating his distributions of happiness or misery to his creatures by the respective degrees of virtue or vice in their conduct and behaviour. It consists not with the majesty or wisdom of the Supreme Lawgiver, to give us laws, without requiring obedience to those laws; nor can his justice suffer them to be violated with impunity.

We are apt indeed to rest our hopes, securely, as we think, on the divine mercy and goodness. The mercy of our Creator

is

is an object that agreeably flatters our wishes, cherishes our hopes, and speaks peace to the soul; and we have a pleasure, therefore, in indulging all such sentiments as represent his mercy like the sun, universal in its influence, rising upon the evil and the good, upon the just and the unjust. God is indeed abundant in goodness, and his mercy is over all his works. Numberless instances we may observe of his goodness and beneficence to his creatures, few of his severity and resentment. His judgments descend slowly upon the worst of sinners, and even then are tempered with mercy. He is as merciful as is consistent with the purity of his nature, or with the honour of his laws: but as his power extends not to impossibilities, but to the proper objects of power; so his mercy is limited to the penitent, the only fit objects of mercy. As a father pitieth his own children, so is the Lord merciful; but it is to them that fear him. His goodness does not express itself in arbitrary grants of pardon to the persevering offender, but

always

always delights to meet and receive the returning penitent. He proposes to make us happy by piety and virtue, not without them; by offering the privileges and blessings of the Christian institution, but not by dispensing with its laws. While we remember his mercy, therefore, let us not forget, that justice and holiness are attributes equally essential to him.

The providence of God, we may in many instances observe, permits, in this world, the best and most faithful of his servants to be involved in various misfortunes, to suffer numerous afflictions, and, on some occasions, the severest tortures. Can we then think, that the JUDGE of all the earth will permit the wicked, those who have rejected his authority, those who must be objects of his displeasure, to escape, here or hereafter, with less severe sufferings, than those to which even the virtuous and good, who are undoubtedly objects of favour, are sometimes exposed in this life? The evils we now see and feel are strong intimations of the possibility of still greater

evils

evils in futurity, and of their confiftency with the divine mercy and goodnefs.

If, then, fin moft affuredly bringeth forth death; if it is pregnant with mifery, and its confequences muft prove inevitably fatal to every perfevering finner; let it be our determined purpofe, not to pay fuch homage to the public opinion, as to live more in fubjection to it, than to the convictions of reafon and confcience. The point to be attended to, is not what conduct may be applauded by others, but what is right, what becomes us as men and as Chriftians; not what the manners of the world may recommend, not what cuftom and fafhion prefcribe, but what the laws of GOD, what confcience and duty fay. In our own breaft fits the monitor whofe fentiments we are above all things to regard. To that monitor, the faithful friend to our happinefs, let us ever pay more deference than to prevailing manners or opinions, and prefer the juft approbation of our own heart to all other applaufe.

If our principles and manners are to be formed and regulated by the example of the world, we may indeed, in some instances, possibly act right: but we must assume different characters; our manners must fluctuate with the manners of the world; and we must comply with every varying mode of virtue or vice, to which the accidental fashion of the day may give a temporary sanction. How much superior he, who, however singular, adheres invariably to the line of duty, uniformly acts the part his heart dictates, scorns any compliances which differ from it, and despises that approbation which is not to be acquired but at the expence of being unfaithful to his God, and unjust to himself?

Let not, then, either example or persuasion, or the fear of censure, or the reproach of singularity, prevail with us to conform to the corruptions of the world. Let us not be timid in virtue, and audacious in vice; fearing the censure of the world, which we might securely disregard; disregarding

regarding the difpleafure of Heaven, which we ought above all things to fear. Let it be our principal care to keep our eye attentively fixed upon the laws of religion, as the rule and guide of our conduct; and if we find, that, by complying with the manners of the world, we have deviated from thofe laws, and loft fight of our duty, and fuffered ourfelves to be carried down with the ftream of any prevailing vice, let us exert our beft efforts to ftem the torrent, and return to that point of duty from which we had departed.

It is indeed with reluctance we are prevailed on to difengage ourfelves from vices, errors, or follies, which we have once adopted, and to which we have adhered: becaufe this cannot be done without a humiliating circumftance; without the fhame of making acknowledgments, to which the natural pride of mankind makes it painful to fubmit. But let no one offer fuch an indignity to God, or to his own underftanding, as to be more afraid of the fhame of acknowledging a wrong practice,

tice, than of the guilt of perſevering in it. However painful it may be to pride, nothing can appear of more eaſy vindication in the eye of reaſon, nothing more praiſeworthy in the ſight of Heaven, than to go off from error, and guilt, and folly, as ſoon as they are diſcovered; and to ſuffer no wrong prepoſſeſſions, no favourite attachments, no perſuaſion, however artful, no authority, however powerful, and no example or cuſtom, however general and prevailing, to enſlave the mind, and detain it from following whitherſoever reaſon, truth, and duty point the way.

For better it is to weigh every action in the balance of truth and reaſon, than in the ſcale of popular opinion; better to retire alone to the narrow, unfrequented, but ſecure walk of virtue, than to go along with the multitude in the broad way that leadeth to deſtruction; better to hazard the reproaches that may attend a virtuous ſingularity, which will hereafter be followed with laſting honours, than to comply with vices and follies which the caprice

caprice of Fashion may have lent a short-lived reputation. Let us remember, that to hold fast our integrity amidst a general corruption, to be singular in goodness amidst public degeneracy, argues the highest moral worth and excellence; and will in a peculiar manner point out and recommend us to the favourable regard of that BEING, whose delight is in the saints that are upon the earth, and in such as excel in virtue.

SERMON IV.

On Conscience.

Job xxvii. 6.

My heart shall not reproach me so long as I live.

WE are by nature formed with a power or faculty which furnishes us with such impressions or sentiments of moral good and evil, that we necessarily give our approbation to the one, and withhold it from the other. A sense of virtue and vice is so closely interwoven in our frame and texture, that our being must be extinguished before that sense can be totally lost. It is this principle, this internal sense,

sense, to which Job in the text expresses his regard, and in conformity to which he determines to act: *My heart shall not reproach me so long as I live.*

In considering which words, I shall observe, *1st*, The nature and office of that principle in us, which is here styled the *heart*; *2dly*, What conduct will secure to us its approbation; and, *lastly*, The happiness resulting from such a conduct.

I. By the *heart* is here meant that moral principle distinguished generally by the name of *conscience*, which points out the distinctions of good and evil, and exhibits to our view the law of our nature, in all the important branches of it, in plain and intelligible characters. It gives us a quick and immediate perception of our duty, and of the rectitude or iniquity of our conduct, without the trouble of deep researches or laboured disquisitions; approves and prompts us to good actions, disapproves and dissuades from others.

That there is such a moral faculty, or directing principle, within us, is evident
beyond

beyond a question. Every man must be conscious, not only of a power, common to him with the inferior creation, of complying with the solicitations of passion or appetite; but also of a superior faculty or power, not possessed by other creatures, that of suppressing the inclinations of a hurtful appetite, of opposing the impulses of a wrong passion, and of forming and regulating his whole conduct by certain laws. Every action is accompanied with a certain consciousness of right or wrong, whereby we become self-approved, or self-reproached.

The moral principle seems designed by the Author of our being to be to the mind what the eye is to the body: and it is its office to direct us in the way in which we should walk; to admonish us of every deviation from it; and to bring us back, whenever we turn aside to the right hand or to the left. It justifies, and applauds, when we do right; reproaches, and condemns, when we act amiss; and gives secret intimations, that we shall accordingly be
justified

justified or condemned at a future tribunal, where we must all one day appear.

This principle is indeed, in particular persons, more or less active and vigorous, according as they have established, or reduced, its influence, by an habitual attention to its admonitions, or by constant efforts to silence and suppress them. If we attend to its suggestions, and follow it as the guide of life, it will lead us on to piety and virtue; if we endeavour to oppose or evade its counsels, its power may be gradually diminished, but never totally lost. There are seasons in which this principle, in spite of all arts and efforts to suppress it, will recover its power; as when the passions have been broken and subdued by adversity, and are succeeded by serious reflections. Conscience will then resume its authority, and execute its office, in laying the obligations of duty before us, and in severe accusations and reproaches for having departed from them.

Having thus considered the nature of
the

the moral principle in us which in the text is styled the *heart*, let us,

II. Observe what conduct will secure to us its approbation.

In order to this, it is necessary that it obtain the supremacy of the mind, and preside over all inferior principles, and regulate and govern every propension and affection of our nature, without being itself controlled or influenced by them. We should reverence it as the oracle of God, the faithful interpreter of his will; and give a constant attention to it, and form our whole conduct by its counsels. In all important points of duty, its decisions will be generally clear; and in particular dubious cases, where it may not be easy to decide upon the lawfulness or unlawfulness of an action, it ought to be a sacred maxim with us, to adhere to that side of the question where our integrity will be most secure, and not to endanger it by too near approaches to sin. Such approaches lead naturally to known and avowed iniquity; for he who can allow him-

himself to hazard an action, the lawfulness of which is not apparent, and the unlawfulness suspected, betrays a propensity which will not permit him long to hesitate at the commission of evident and undisputed crimes.

But further: To secure the approbation of our heart, we must not only religiously follow its guidance, and observe its dictates; but it is necessary also to acquire a just information in our duty, and to acquaint ourselves with its obligations. For conscience itself may be erroneous, and hold out false lights; and then, however faithfully we pursue its directions, this will not always insure our innocence. St Paul styles himself the least of the apostles, not meet to be called an apostle, and the chief of sinners, because he persecuted the church of Christ,—though, as he himself informs us, he did it in ignorance. Though we ought to act agreeably to our convictions, in complying with the dictates of an erroneous conscience, and it would be highly culpable

culpable in us to disregard them whilst we believed them to be right; yet if such were not inevitable errors, but the effects of voluntary corruption or negligence, they must subject us to the imputation of guilt, and consequently to the reproaches of our own mind, as soon as light enough is let in upon it, to give it a just discernment of its errors, and of the criminal occasions of them.

If, therefore, we would secure the approbation of our heart, it must be our equal care to inform ourselves of our duty, and to live up to our information.

III. Let us, lastly, consider the happiness resulting from such a conduct.

1*st*, The testimony of the heart in our favour is a secret intimation, suggested by nature, that the JUDGE of the whole earth will concur with such testimony, and affirm the judgment which our heart has formed. *If our heart condemn us not, we may have confidence towards God.* For virtue and vice, good and evil, must appear to be such to GOD as well as to men:

with

with this difference, that his supreme wisdom always beholds the reality of things with an unerring **eye, and with** infallible certainty sees **them** to be **what they are;** whilst our imperfect sight **is often** deceived by appearances and illusi**ons, and b**etrayed into various errors. Pa**ssions and preju**dices may corrupt our **understanding, and** extort a partial **judgment. The most** iniquitous may give themselves a false applause for weak or **superstitious** services; and, on the other hand, the most virtuous and pious minds may be sometimes alarmed with **terrors and** despondencies that are **visionary** and groundless.

But in such cases, **Reason is not** consulted, but neglected; **our judgment is** not **the judgment of our** reason, **but of** our **passions: it is not Reason which ac**quits **or condemns; it is Fear, Ignorance,** Superstition, **or Melancholy, which usurp** its place. **Conscience forms its judgment by** comparing **our conduct with** the law **of** our duty; **but** superstitious imaginations and melancholy fears have **no** rule of judgment; and often determine against the most evident rules, both of reason and revelation. But where Reason's voice is heard, and no passions or prepossessions are permitted to overrule its authority; where the mind has duly considered and examined our conduct by the laws of GOD, and pronounces a deliberate, uninfluenced sentence; this sentence, we have the best grounds to believe, will be affirmed at the heavenly tribunal, and may encourage us to look up with confidence to our Supreme JUDGE, in just expectation of his approbation and favour.

But further: The approbation of our heart not only opens to us the prospect of a distant felicity, and gives us an assurance of the future favour of Heaven; but also diffuses through the mind a present serenity and satisfaction. The Author of our being has appointed internal peace and tranquillity to be the immediate reward of obedience to the laws of our nature: And a reward it is that well deserves our attention. This is the state to which Philoso-
phy

phy pretended to conduct her followers, as the summit of human enjoyment, the nearest approach to happiness we can make in this life. But to this state Religion will most effectually lead us, and to these paths of peace will be our best and surest guide.

Nothing can be more pleasurable to the mind, than to reflect, that our conduct has been such as reason and conscience have dictated and approved; that we have acted in conformity to the laws of our MAKER, and have lived up to the design of our creation. If, upon a just scrutiny into our actions, we find, that, as far as human infirmity permits, we have endeavoured to be faithful in our duty to GOD, and to pay that reverence and submission which are due from all intellectual beings to the FATHER of the universe: if we find that integrity, equity, fidelity, and benevolence, have been the rules of our behaviour to our fellow-creatures; and that our passions have been, if not always, yet generally, under due government:—

if such is the result of our enquiry, we need not labour to work in ourselves a conviction that we have acted right; for peace and complacency will spontaneously spring up from it. Our nature is so framed and constituted, that it is impossible not to receive self-gratulations from the consciousness of such behaviour.

This consciousness affords a most lasting and secure satisfaction: which is not, like other pleasures, limited to certain seasons or conjunctures; does not change with circumstance, nor satiate with repetition, nor grow old with time; but continues as long as the consciousness that gave it birth; and has this peculiar advantage, that it may be enjoyed in its highest perfection, when we can enjoy nothing else,—when the body sickens, and its senses languish and decay.

Which leads me to observe, lastly, That the satisfaction of a self-approving heart is most sensibly felt at the most awful period of our lives, at a juncture when all other pleasures

pleasures forsake us,—at the approach of our dissolution.

If in that situation we can recal the transactions of former days, and of the years that are past, and suffer them to appear in review before us; and can observe, that our deportment has, upon the whole, been formed and regulated by the monitions of conscience; that no corrupt passions have been more attended to than its counsels; that our habitual care has been to know and do the will of our MAKER, to consult his honour, the good of our fellow-creatures, and our own eternal felicity; that whatever particular failings and infirmities we may have been subject to, yet that the general and uniform course of our life has been conducted with uprightness and integrity;—we must doubtless receive a peculiar satisfaction, a deep-felt joy, a joy which cannot be described, and which the heart of the virtuous and good alone can conceive. We shall not then be afraid to encounter the last enemy of our nature, Death; which will be difarmed of its terrors, and no longer formidable. The grave we fhall confider as the gate to immortality, as introductory to that ftate where confcious integrity gives the beft-grounded hopes of the approbation and favour of our MAKER.

And what can our conceptions form to us more defireable, than to have confolation adminiftered in that hour of diftrefs, when nature moft needs it? to have fecret infufions of joy poured in upon the foul, and to have relief fupplied from within, when all outward affiftance is vain? How inexpreffible muft be the fatisfaction, to have no guilty fears at that time to fix a fting in our bofom! to have the pains of difeafe mitigated by an internal compofure! to be able to look back upon this world without remorfe, and into the next without terror! to have confidence towards GOD, a confidence that that all gracious BEING, whofe laws it has been our habitual care to obey, whofe favour has been our firft object, is about to reward our

our obedience with joys unspeakable and full of glory; and that he who has been our Patron and Protector in life, will be our Guide and Guardian through the vale of death, and an inseparable Friend and Father to us in our journey through eternity!

Who then would not wish to live the life of the righteous, that his last end may be like his; perplexed by no unrepented sins, disturbed by no painful reproaches, distracted by no guilty apprehensions; but supported by conscious goodness, by hopes full of immortality, and by such anticipations of the heavenly felicity as are next to the possession of it?

From what has been offered, it may appear, that the moral principle which we call *conscience*, and is in the text styled the *heart*, was given us to be the guide of our conduct, and to lead us to an obedience to the laws of GOD, with which our own happiness is inseparably connected. Be it then our first and principal care, to be ever attentive to the friendly voice of this
domestic

domestic guide, this faithful monitor within us. Let it be our equal endeavour to inform ourselves of the duties required from us, and to live suitably to our informations. Such a conduct will secure to us the approbation of our heart; will diffuse a lasting serenity through our whole life; will supply us with the happiest consolations at the hour of death; will recommend us to the approbation of the Divine BEING; and will procure the most inestimable of all blessings, a gracious sentence at the final judgment.

SERMON V.

HOUSE of MOURNING.

ECCLES. vii. 4.

The heart of the wise is in the house of mourning.

THIS is the sentiment of one of the wisest and greatest of the sons of men; one who, to superior abilities of mind, added the most ample possessions of fortune; one who had all the pleasures of the world at his command, and of all had made the fullest experience. *Whatever mine eyes desired,* says he, *I kept not from them; I withheld not my heart from any joy, till I might see what was that good for the sons of men*

men which they should do under heaven all the days of their life. The result of his various experiments and inquiries after happiness was, that riches, honour, power, pleasure, every thing, was vain, but Religion and Virtue. At his first setting out in the world, he was inclined to search for happiness where appearances most promise it, in scenes of mirth and festivity. He said in his heart, *Go to now, I will prove thee with mirth; therefore enjoy pleasure.* But further observation and experience taught him, that *sorrow was better than laughter:* i. e. that it is fitter for creatures, in such a situation as we are here, to be serious and considerate, than dissipated and mirthful; that the former disposition is better suited to our present state, and more conducive to our future felicity, than the latter. Upon this account he determines that *the heart of the wise is in the house of mourning, and the heart of fools in the house of mirth;* i. e. that more valuable and lasting advantages may be derived from attending to scenes of sorrow and adversity, than

than from a life devoted to dissipation and pleasure.

Let us then consider this decision, and inquire into the reasons of the preference given by the Royal Preacher to the former.

The natural inclinations of mankind, indeed, plead strongly in favour of pleasure; but however inviting the prospect, however flattering the idea, they who make pleasure their sole object will seldom fail to find, that the disappointment of their hopes will lead them at last to the conclusion of Solomon, that *all is vanity*. The perpetual unremitting pursuit of pleasure has, besides, a tendency almost imperceptibly to seduce, and to lead the mind gradually astray from what ought to be its first and principal object. Religion, it is true, was not meant to afflict or oppress, but to render mankind universally as happy as the state of the world will permit; and it has issued out no prohibitions against innocent pleasures, which are far from being incompatible with a proper regard

gard to duty. But it ought to be considered, that pleasures, when so far indulged as to be admitted to take possession of the whole heart, to exclude an intermixture of serious sentiments, and leave no room for hours of religious and virtuous reflection, though not criminal in themselves, lead often to unhappy consequences.

On this account, adversity has ever been reputed the school in which are given the best instructions in wisdom; in which few are made worse, many become wiser and better. On the contrary, how few are reformed or improved, what numbers are seduced and corrupted, by the lessons of prosperity! Of the danger of which, even to the wisest and best, the Psalmist was himself an eminent instance. He who could so well instruct others concerning the uncertainty and vanity of the world and its enjoyments, yet in his prosperity could not only indulge the vainest of thoughts, and say, he should never be removed, but was tempted also to perpetrate the worst of crimes. But, in his adversity, how

does

does he reproach himself for the guilt of his pleasurable hours, and acknowledge, that it was good for him that he had been in trouble, and that God of very faithfulness had caused him to be troubled! for *before I was afflicted*, says he, *I went wrong, but now have I kept thy word.*

In a round of pleasures, we are apt to become too unmindful of what we owe to God, and too neglectful of the debts of mercy due to our suffering brethren. Pleasure and prosperity are fatal seducers; and, when we give ear to their counsels, lead to such a train of dissipations, such a succession of follies and vices, that it has been justly observed, that the greatest misfortune which can befal us, is, never to meet misfortune. We have reason, then, to adore the wisdom of Providence, that has appointed all the vicissitudes to which we are subject; that has chequered human life with good and evil; and has planned out a succession of various cares and troubles, for beings who are little capable of

supporting,

supporting, in a rational manner, a state of total pleasure and prosperity.

On this account it is, that Solomon determines the preference in favour of the house of mourning: for there the heart is made better;—there it becomes more serious, more susceptive of every tender, every religious impression. How mild, and candid, and reasonable, may we observe mankind; how open to virtuous reflection, how disposed to sentiments of benevolence and compassion; whilst they are feeling their own, or the afflictions of others! but how inattentive often, and how insensible to others sufferings, when in the midst of prosperity, and in full pursuit of pleasure!

Too seldom do They, who amidst ease, affluence, and indulgence, withhold not their heart from any joy; too, too seldom do they reflect, how many unhappy beings are wearing out life amidst the difficulties and labours of poverty, or the pangs and tortures of disease, whilst they bestow not perhaps the smallest portion of their abundance

dance to alleviate the sufferings of their possibly not less deserving, but more unfortunate, brethren!

But, on the other hand, scenes of adversity awaken our compassion, correct that levity which is the inlet to vice, form us to consideration, soften the heart, and give us a taste for the serious pleasures of Benevolence and Humanity. By being acquainted with grief, we learn to feel for the unhappy; we learn, that a pleasurable indulgence of ourselves, and an insensibility to the sufferings of others, are by no means suited to such a state of things as is here before us; and that every tender regard is due to the numerous wants and sorrows of the afflicted.

Would we permit ourselves to view the world in a true light,—in the light in which, not only as good Christians, but as wise men, we ought;—we should learn, that it was not designed merely for the purposes of festivity and entertainment; and that Providence never meant to place us in it, as he did the leviathan in the waters,

ters, only to take our paſtime therein. The world is to be conſidered as a ſchool of diſcipline and inſtruction, (to ſome a ſevere one), intended to train and educate us for a future, better, and more permanent ſtate. Fain would we, indeed, have it to be a ſcene of enjoyment, a region of mirth and pleaſure: but experience tells us, that it is to many a vale of tears; to the moſt fortunate, a chequered ſcene of good and evil; and that none of us can, nor (we may preſume) is it fit we ſhould, enjoy any conſiderable portion of felicity upon earth. It would incline us to think it good for us to be here; would withdraw our attention and affections too much from the next world, and too much attach them to the preſent.

The infinitely wiſe CREATOR of the world has appointed us to be born to trouble; has intermingled afflictions with every ſtage and ſtation of life; has decreed pleaſure and pain, like day and night, to ſucceed each other in conſtant rotation:— with a view, it ſhould ſeem, to intimate, that

that he reserves our enjoyment of complete fulness of felicity to another state; and that here our principal cares should be employed in endeavouring to render ourselves worthy of happiness, by our endeavours to impart it, by ministering to the wants, healing the sorrows, alleviating and softening, as much as may be, the pains and sufferings of the afflicted.

What then shall we determine ought to be the object of our choice, and which is, upon the whole, the preferable pursuit? Shall we, regardless of other considerations, frequent only the house of mirth, give our whole attention to the enjoyments of life, and to a selfish pursuit of pleasure? or shall we, wisely considerate, extend our views beyond ourselves? Shall we open our hearts to our fellow-beings? Shall we sometimes visit the house of Mourning, and attend with humanity to the complaints of Sorrow? Shall we cultivate a spirit of goodness, beneficence, and charity; and thus make both ourselves, and all within our circle of influence, as happy as our own powers, the state of the world, and the condition of our nature, will permit? Which is the more eligible satisfaction,—To gratify a short-lived passion, to snatch a transient gleam of mirth; or to enjoy that continued sunshine of delight we feel, when we dry up the tears of the distressed, and bind up the wounds of the sorrowful; when we raise the dejected head, and comfort the afflicted heart; when we become fathers to the fatherless, and cause the widow's heart to sing for joy? Far, far superior is the inward complacency, the heart-felt satisfaction, resulting from such acts of mercy, to all the giddy joy, and all the dissolute pleasure, that the house of mirth, or the gayest festivity, can inspire.

The human heart was purposely framed with such an happy sensibility by its MAKER, that, when unvitiated, it has a secret pleasure in sympathetic sorrows, and is itself relieved by imparting relief to others; and has, perhaps, a truer delight even in sharing the afflictions of the un-

for-

fortunate, and weeping with those that weep, than can be found in the indulgence of any sensual or selfish passion.

If such, then, be the advantages which may be derived from attending to scenes of sorrow, Solomon might, in a moral or religious view, justly give them a preference to the house of mirth. But though this in general be true, yet prudence is requisite in the application of this, as of other instructions; lest, as is the too common foible of our nature, in order to avoid one, we run inconsiderately into the error of another extreme. It is not to be understood, that the prudent and good should confine their conversation to the house of mourning; or that all are imprudent who entertain themselves with mirth; or that pleasure is inconsistent, either with the reason of a wise, or the religion of a good, man. Religion may have a serious, not an austere aspect; is not of a severe and rigid disposition; rejects no pleasures, but such as are criminal and hurtful, and excess in others that become hurtful
merely

merely by excess. There is not a single pleasure worthy of a rational being, that is not, within certain limits, consistent with religion and virtue. The office of wisdom and religion is only to take care that our pleasures interfere not with any present duty, nor be the occasion of any future sorrow or remorse.

And accordingly the whole design of the text is, to give mankind an admonition, which indeed they often want, that the present is not a state in which they should purpose to attach and devote themselves solely to festivity and pleasure. The scenes that every day present themselves, are far from leading to such a dissipated turn of mind. Consideration, on the contrary, is the great law of our nature, the first principle of wisdom and right conduct. Often ought we to call our ways to remembrance; to consider in what manner we have performed our duty to God and our fellow-creatures; how we have conducted ourselves in prosperity, how felt and relieved the afflictions of those in adversity;

what

what has been our behaviour in these respects, and what account we shall one day give of it.

The admission of such reflections, far from laying a burden upon the spirits, would be the best method to relieve them; far from leading us into the paths of sorrow, would be the surest guide to tranquillity and peace of mind. For a rational, permanent tranquillity of mind, is the result of virtuous consideration, the prerogative of innocence, the attendant and reward of religion; for religion is so far from taking it away, that nothing else can give it. The common amusements and dissipations of the world serve rather to relax our cares, to suspend a sense of uneasiness, and to have the effect of opiates, in creating a short forgetfulness of pain, than to supply any permanent or substantial enjoyment. The world has not a more valuable and lasting pleasure, than that serene joy of heart which arises from the consciousness of having acquitted ourselves as we ought, and from the consequent

sequent well grounded hopes of the favour and approbation of our all-gracious MAKER and JUDGE.

Would you then possess pure and genuine pleasure? seek it in the paths of virtue. Would you enjoy true felicity; Do you enquire, with the Psalmist, *Who will shew us any good?* From him learn where it is to be found: *Lord, lift thou up the light of thy countenance upon us.* It is GOD alone, the Fountain of happiness, that can convey it to his creatures; but will most certainly convey it to none but the virtuous, the benevolent, the merciful, and the good.

SERMON VI.

Positive Institutions inferior to Moral Duties.

MATTH. xxiii. 23.

Wo unto you, Scribes and Pharisees, *hypocrites! for ye pay tithe of* mint, and anise, and cummin; and have omitted the weightier matters of the law, judgment, mercy, and faith: these ought ye to have done, and not to leave the other undone.

OUR SAVIOUR, in these words, reproves the ostentatious hypocrisy of the Scribes and Pharisees, who were zealously punctual in the observance of all external and ritual duties, and scrupulously exact

exact in paying tithes of herbs of small confideration,—whilft they neglected moral duties, which were of much greater importance, and omitted the weightier matters of the law, judgment, mercy, and faith. The former ought not to be left undone; but the latter, as our Lord afferts, demand our principal attention, and ought to be the firft objects of our care.

The text is, then, a general determination, which leaves no room to doubt what is the moft fubftantial and important part of religion, by exprefsly refolving it into moral rectitude, and integrity of life and manners.

I fhall endeavour to illuftrate this decifion of our Lord, by fhowing, that moral duties are the weightier matters of the law, and in their nature more important, in their obligation more neceffary, than ritual injunctions; and fhall conclude with fome obfervations from the doctrine in the text. And,

I. The moral duties are thofe which reafon teaches us to be due to God, our neighbour,

neighbour, and ourselves; which are of eternal and necessary obligation, and have in their nature an intrinsic and immutable rectitude: Such are piety, justice, mercy, fidelity, benevolence, temperance, and the like. Positive institutions are such as have in them no intrinsic or immutable excellence; but are only occasionally appointed, and receive their whole authority from the command of the legislature: Such were circumcision, sacrifices, and other ritual observances, among the Jews; and such are baptism and the eucharist under the Christian dispensation. These duties, indeed, claim our strictest attention and observance, as they are enjoined by the Supreme Lawgiver, for wise purposes; but yet are not to be reputed of equal importance or obligation with the moral duties.

God has instituted some external rites and ceremonies to be observed, in order to aid and confirm our natural approbation and esteem of virtue, to remind us of its obligations, and to incline and habituate us to the practice of it. He has also proposed

proposed some doctrines to our faith, with the same religious view and tendency. But it cannot be the chief and principal aim of religion to make us proselytes to speculative opinions, or exterior observances. We dishonour the wisdom of GOD, if we suppose that he can command us to pursue any thing more than those duties in which he has taught us to discern the highest worth and excellence; or that he can require us to oppose the inward sense and perception of our minds, and contradict that moral faculty which himself gave us to guide our feet, and to be a light unto our paths.

The pre-eminence of moral duties above ritual injunctions will appear, if we consider the absolute goodness of the Divine BEING; and that the felicity of his creatures is the principal object of the whole administration of his providence, and of every law to which he requires our obedience. It is evident, then, that a religion of divine institution must be chiefly framed with a view to engage our observance of of those duties which are most essential to human happiness; such as piety, and the social virtues of benevolence, justice, fidelity. For to these virtues life is indebted for its principal satisfactions and enjoyments. They are the true sources of both private and public tranquillity. If, then, these are the occasions and instruments of human happiness, it may reasonably be inferred, that God, who desires our happiness, would have a principal regard to them in the laws which he requires us to observe; and would give them the preference above other duties, which have not so direct and immediate a tendency to the end of his creation and government,—the felicity of his creatures.

II. Ritual or ceremonial injunctions must be considered as subordinate to moral duties; because the latter are the end for which the former were instituted, and the end must be acknowledged to be more valuable and excellent than the means. The supreme excellence and perfection, as well as the final happiness of our nature, is founded

founded on moral virtue: this, confequently, ought to be our principal view; and every thing elfe muft derive its value from its fubferviency to this end. Ritual inftitutions are well adapted to this our infant and imperfect ftate; and, as they remind us of the obligations of religion, fupport us in that uniform exercife of virtue, and increafe our love to GOD and our neighbour, are religiously to be obferved. They are ufeful as means to produce and preferve in us a good and pious frame of mind: but where they are ineffectual to thefe purpofes (as we too often fuffer them to be), they lofe their value; they are then *precepts by which men fhall not live*, as the prophet has expreffed it.

III. The fuperiority and pre-eminence of moral virtue may further appear from hence, that the obligation and exercife of it will continue for ever; whereas all ceremonial obfervances are in their nature only temporary. *Charity*, fays Paul, *never faileth*; which is one reafon of the preference he gives it above faith and hope. The

The pious difpofitions of the foul will not decay nor die with us; but will be continued, improved, perfected, and perpetuated in heaven. The fame goodnefs and benevolence of mind which conftitute our principal excellence and happinefs here on earth, will continue to be our higheft perfection and felicity in every future period of our being. From hence, then, may appear the dignity and pre-eminence of moral virtue, when compared with ritual obfervances, which are meant to be affiftances and fupports to religion, only during the infancy and imperfection of our being; and muft ceafe when we arrive at a ftate of greater improvement and maturity in another life: whereas the moral virtues will conduct and accompany us to heaven; will be the brighteft gems in our celeftial crown, and the higheft ornaments of our moft elevated ftate.

IV. The fcriptures every where reprefent the moral virtues as of the firft importance, and the chief end of all religion. GOD did indeed prefcribe to the Jews a
pompous

pompous service, and a numerous train of rituals, adapted to the genius and circumstances of that people, and meant to preserve them from the barbarous idolatries of their neighbour nations, by indulging them in innocent ceremonies of their own. But, even under that dispensation, these were of inferior importance, when compared to justice, truth, integrity, and mercy: and when they were not accompanied with those moral duties, we find that God rejected even his own institutions; oblations were vain, and the multitude of their sacrifices to no purpose.

The great intention of the Gospel is so evidently to engage men in the practice of virtue, and to produce in them all the fruits of righteousness, mercy, and peace, that it is almost unnecessary to produce particular passages to this purpose. Our SAVIOUR and his apostles every where inculcate piety and virtue, the love of GOD and man; and represent them as the substance of all religion: they teach us to consider external observances only as means

to

to assist us in attaining these divine virtues, which constitute the happiness and perfection of human nature.

I proceed to some observations deducible from this doctrine. And,

1st, We may from hence see the propriety and necessity of frequent exhortations to the practice of moral duties. Moral duties seem to be held in small estimation by some persons, who consider them as of the lowest importance in religion, and as fitter subjects of instruction from a heathen philosopher, than from a disciple of the gospel of CHRIST. But such opinions have no foundation in reason or scripture; for we have seen, that they both agree in representing the moral duties, as what GOD chiefly values and requires, and what therefore ought principally to be taught and inculcated. These our SAVIOUR himself, and his Apostles, constantly urged and recommended as the great aim and end of religion. Our SAVIOUR came into the world to teach men *to live righteously, soberly, and godly, in this present world.* The Apostles, in all their discourses, pursued the moral plan of their great Master; and every servant of CHRIST ought undoubtedly to tread in the same steps, and inculcate the same duties.

2*dly,* We may observe how perfectly the Christian revelation corresponds with the voice of Nature, in asserting the importance and excellence of moral virtues, and placing them in the first rank of its duties. And this circumstance, though not of itself, without other evidence, sufficient to evince the truth and divine original of the gospel, yet at least entitles it to attention and favour; and must incline all the friends of virtue to wish well to an institution calculated to establish a general integrity of manners, and to promote the moral rectitude, perfection, and universal happiness, of human nature. The intrinsic excellence of the Christian system, therefore, gives it a just claim to peculiar regard: for the more any institution of religion improves and advances

moral

moral rectitude, the more it exalts and dignifies human nature, and is confequently the more worthy of GOD; for which reafon the advocates for Chriftianity have wifely infifted on the amiablenefs, purity, and excellence, of its morals, as ftrong prefumptive marks of its heavenly original.

If, indeed, we fhould conceive of the religion of CHRIST as infifting chiefly on an affent to points of fpeculation, or the obfervance of external rites,—it will not in this light appear fo divine and excellent, fo worthy of GOD, or fo well adapted to the wants and neceffities of his creatures, as in thofe accounts which our SAVIOUR and his Apoftles have given of it.

3*dly*, and laftly, From hence we may learn to be efpecially careful in obferving the duties of integrity, piety, juftice, mercy, and the like. Let us not conclude, that we are religious, becaufe we are right in our faith, or punctual in our attendance on public worfhip. Thefe are indeed excellent and neceffary means and helps

helps to religion; but religion itself is seated in the mind, and consists in that reverence and obedience of heart to GOD, and those upright and friendly dispositions towards men, which those means are intended to produce and promote in us. But as when, upon a comparison of two objects, one is found to be less important than the other, we are often weak enough to consider it as scarce of any importance at all, it is highly necessary to remind ourselves, that we ought not to presume to neglect or disregard any institutions of divine appointment; that our obligations to obey all GOD's commands whatever, are absolute and indispensable; and that commands merely positive, admitted to be from him, lay us under the strictest obligation to observe them, and are not to be slighted or undervalued under a pretence that they are in their nature and importance inferior to morality.

Let us be careful, then, to pay a due regard to positive precepts, as they are enjoined by the authority of HIM to whom
we

we owe all obedience, and as they are wisely framed for the improvement and establishment of virtue: but let us remember, that moral rectitude and goodness are the weightier matters of the law; that *these are to be done, and the other not to be left undone.*

SERMON VII.

Goodness of God in the Redemption.

1 JOHN iv. 10.

Herein is love, not that we loved God, but that he loved us, and sent his Son to be the propitiation for our sins.

THAT God, the Creator of all things, is a Being merciful and gracious, benignant and compassionate,—is a truth which nature dictates, and was generally understood and acknowledged even in the Gentile world. Nor need we wonder, that they who are left to the sole investigations of reason, unassisted by revealed instructions, should yet form so just a conception

ception of the Divine nature. The goodness of the DEITY is visible in that prevalence of good which is apparent in his works; in the common administration of providence; in the face of nature; in our own frame; and in the frame of all things around us.

The Sacred Writings speak the same language with the voice of nature in this particular;—and assure us, That GOD is good to all: That his tender mercies are over all his works: that his goodness extends, not only to those whose obedience and virtue might make them hope to be considered as proper objects of it; but even to the disobedient and undeserving, whom he invites to obedience by repeated mercies, to whom he never refuses forgiveness when they return to duty.

But the divine goodness has not only been amply displayed in the works of creation, and in the conduct of providence, but also in the redemption of mankind; which shall be the subject of our present thoughts.

GOD, the original author and giver of every good gift, hath with a liberal hand conferred his bleffings upon every creature he hath made, according to its capacity, and to the ftation and rank allotted it, and as far as was conducive to the end which his fupreme wifdom intended. But when we have furveyed and confidered all the various meafures of goodnefs diftributed to other creatures, we fhall find a ftill ampler portion of it confpicuous in the nature of Man, whom his CREATOR has placed in a higher rank, and invefted with more eminent privileges and prerogatives, than the reft of the vifible creation. For even in the formation of our corporeal frame, of *this tabernacle of clay, this earthly houfe* (as the apoftle calls it), he feems to have expreffed a peculiar attention to the human fpecies, who excel all other creatures even in exterior appearance,—in erectnefs of ftature, gracefulnefs of form, and in the conftruction and difpofition of every part, for ornament, convenience, and mutual affiftance.

But

But these, it must be acknowledged, are the least of the favours conferred by the Divine bounty. Man's principal glory consists in being formed after the likeness and image of his MAKER, *i. e.* in being invested with moral and intellectual powers; for these are properly the resemblances of the DEITY, whereby man may in some sense be said to participate of the divine nature. Impossible it is, that this image or likeness of GOD should consist in our outward form or construction: but it consists rather in the rational faculties of the soul; or, most of all, in the moral rectitude of those faculties.

This image, then, of GOD, according to which man is said to be formed, must be considered as an expression denoting, that man, in his original formation, was of an order superior to all other animal beings till then created; and was endowed with a power of conforming his nature to that of the ALMIGHTY, in the frame of his spirit, and in the rectitude of his actions: not that man could ever presume to be holy as GOD is holy, or perfect as HE is perfect; but that infinitely holy and good BEING could not fet his feal on any intellectual part of creation, but the impreffion would be in fome degree like himfelf,—good and holy alfo.

Such was Man, fuch the rectitude of his mind and will, fuch his fimilitude to his MAKER, in his primeval ftate, as he originally came forth, pure and immaculate, from the hands of his CREATOR. Reafon then fat at the helm undifturbed; and fteered according to the calm dictates of the Underftanding,—fubject to no tempeftuous commotions from appetites or paffions. He had no enemy within to contend with,—the fenfitive powers being obedient to the intellectual; no law in his members oppofing the law of his mind; no licentious paffions warring againft the authority and government of Reafon. A beam of light, a ray of divine wifdom, fhone upon his underftanding, which difcovered to him the rule of life. There was a harmony between his reafon

and

and affections; an original righteousness; so that it seemed much more easy for him to persevere in a faithful observance of the precept given by his MAKER for the trial of his obedience, than to depart from it, and listen to the persuasions of the tempter.

But man, by unhappily perverting his powers, and transgressing the laws of his CREATOR, incurred the divine displeasure, and became subject to death,—the consequence denounced to transgression. And as all men sinned, the wages of sin became due to all. For it being at all times our most reasonable duty to pay an universal obedience to the laws of GOD, every violation of those laws justly exposed the offender to the punishment due to his transgression.

But though man became a wilful sinner by the perversion of his liberty, and by a voluntary self-depravation; yet as the frailty of his nature laid him open to deception and transgression, the FATHER of our Being looked with an eye of compassion, and

and confidered him as a fit object of mercy; for *he knew whereof we were made, and remembered that we were but duſt.* He was pleaſed, therefore, to extend his compaſſion to our fallen nature: and the effect of this compaſſion was, the miſſion of his Son into the world, to be a propitiation for our ſins; and, by the oblation of himſelf, to make a full and ſufficient ſacrifice and ſatisfaction for the ſins of the world. For our ſakes, the Son of God deſcended from the heavens, and dwelt upon earth; took our nature into a cloſe and intimate union with his own; publiſhed the gracious terms of his covenant, and ſealed it with his blood; by the effuſion and oblation of which, he made an atonement for our ſins, paid the penalty due for our iniquities, and bore the burden of an offending world.

God ſo loved the world, that he gave up his Son; and the Son ſo loved the world, that he gave up himſelf, for our ſalvation. If we contemplate the Son of God, reſigning the inconceivable glory which

which he poffeffed with the FATHER before the foundation of the world; paffing thro' a gradation of humiliation and fufferings; condefcending to unite himfelf to our nature, in its loweft form, and moft afflicted ftate:—if we attend him through the various fcenes of his paffion, fhedding in his agony drops of blood, dragged to crucifixion by a barbarous multitude, expofed as an object of public derifion, the fcorn of the malicious, and fport of the infolent; his facred head infulted with the impious mockery of a crown of thorns; himfelf affixed to the painful crofs, reviled and blafphemed, bleeding and expiring, fuffering every indignity and every torture, in order to reconcile to GOD thofe his creatures, who had forfeited every claim to favour:—we cannot but acknowledge it to be an amazing proof of the moft affectionate goodnefs; we muft be loft in wonder at the riches of his mercy; we muft feel a powerful conviction, that never was love like this love, nor compaffion like that of our REDEEMER.

O all-gracious SAVIOUR of mankind! what words can exprefs the gratitude we owe! How inadequate to thy mercies are our adorations! The tongues of men and angels can but imperfectly praife thee. Thou haft redeemed us by thy blood out of every kindred, and tongue, and people, and nation: For this caufe, at thy name, which is above every name, every knee fhall bow; for worthy art thou to receive blefling, and glory, and honour, and power, for ever and ever.

What has been obferved, may fuggeft the following reflections.

1*ft*, We may from hence learn, how dreadful an evil, and how offenfive to GOD, fin is, which nothing but the blood of his SON could expiate; and how neceffary and indifpenfable is religious obedience, to render us fit objects of divine mercy. In order to be the propitiation for our fins, the SON of GOD, who was fo high in the glory of his FATHER, fubmitted to the loweft circumftances of humanity, fuffered an ignominious and painful

ful death; not the death of a common transgressor, but one reserved by the Romans for the worst and most flagitious of criminals.

The death of CHRIST is in scripture represented to be in the strictest sense a propitiatory sacrifice. The essence of a propitiatory sacrifice consists in this, that the guilt of the sinner is transferred to the victim, and the one is substituted and suffers in the place of the other. If, then, GOD, when about to display the extent of his goodness, and the riches of his mercy, in the remission of our sins, would yet accept no less ransom, no meaner expiation, than the sufferings and sacrifice of his SON, what prospect or hope can we have of escaping the resentments of his justice, if we still persist in disobedience? For let us remember, that the benefits of our Redeemer's sufferings extend only to the penitent and reformed, not to the presumptuous and persevering offender. And if we are not careful to avail ourselves of these sufferings; if we presume to despise the

the mercies of this covenant; if we neglect this greatest, last salvation, this last effort of Divine Goodness to save us;—there remains no further expiation, no more sacrifice for sin, no other Redeemer to suffer, no new covenant to be made. The SON of God will be no Saviour to us; the blood of CHRIST, that fountain of mercy, will for us flow in vain, and be insufficient to wash away the stains and pollution of our guilt.

2*dly*, If GOD so loved us, as to appoint and accept the death of his SON as an expiatory sacrifice, by which all past and forsaken sins are forgiven, and we are readmitted to the divine favour; we ought also, in imitation of the divine goodness, to be kind, tender-hearted, forgiving one another, as GOD for CHRIST's sake hath forgiven us. We are by nature equal, fellow-servants of the same Lord, heirs of the same hopes; and the widest distinctions of birth, wealth, power, or station, place us at no great distance one from another. The indignities or injuries, therefore, we
may

may receive from our fellow-creatures, can in the meafure of their guilt bear no proportion to the offences we commit againſt the infinite SOVEREIGN of the Univerſe; by whoſe power we ſubſiſt, and on whoſe mercy we depend; to whom we owe our being, and all the bleſſings that attend it; who daily helpeth us, and poureth his benefits upon us, and hath engaged us to him by various wonders of love, and repeated miracles of mercy.

If, then, GOD forgives our ſins, thus heightened and aggravated by ſo many conſiderations of goodneſs; and forgives them in a manner ſo expreſſive of his affection, as to appoint his SON to be the victim in our ſtead; what violence or injuries can we receive one from another, that ought not to claim forgiveneſs from us? Since our heavenly FATHER is thus merciful to us, how ought we to be merciful one to another?

But how widely different from this precept of our LORD, is the too general practice of thoſe who aſſume the name of his followers!

followers! Instead of kind affections, and friendly offices, how willing are we, too often, to seize the opportunities that offer, of repaying injuries with injuries, and of rendering evil for evil! How prone to approve, how prompt to execute, every dictate of revenge! But with a behaviour so repugnant to the precepts and example of our benevolent REDEEMER, how can we hope to participate in the mercies and blessings he has purchased for us? how can we lift up our eyes to implore his mediation? What self-condemnation must we feel from a comparison of our own conduct with that of our blessed LORD! How ought we to fear, lest he for ever turn away his eyes from those whose dispositions and manners are so much the reverse of his own!

Lastly, Let us reflect, that this inestimable blessing, this mighty salvation wrought for us, calls for our sincerest acknowledgments, and the most devout sacrifices of praise and thanksgiving to GOD the author, and to JESUS the voluntary minister,

minister, of this dispensation of mercy. Let us express our acknowledgments in a grateful and inviolable obedience to every injunction of this great PRESERVER of souls. What better return can we make to the ALMIGHTY, than, with hearts deeply affected by a just sense of the greatness of his mercy, to pay our highest tribute of adoration to him who was so gracious, as not only at our creation to impress on the human mind the image of his own goodness,—and thus to render us in some sense partakers of the divine nature, and of all the happiness consequent upon it; but also, when we had defaced this image, had plunged ourselves in sin and misery, and saw extinguished all hopes of ever arriving at that state of perfection and felicity for which we were originally designed,—was pleased to restore us to a new capacity of happiness, by sending his SON into the world, to take our nature and our guilt upon him, and to make an atonement for the sins of mankind?

This paternal goodness of GOD demands from his creatures every expression of filial love; and this love is to be expressed, as the Apostle informs us, in keeping his commandments. We are to love his law, we are to delight in conforming to his will, we are to obey his precepts; not from constraint, not barely from a conviction of our obligations, and a sense of duty to him; but our sense of duty must be animated by an affection to his service, by a love of obedience, and the most grateful sentiments of his goodness to us, particularly in our redemption.

May we, then, never render in vain the incarnation and sufferings of our REDEEMER; may we never by our sins disappoint the gracious intentions of his mercy; may we form our lives and manners by his example and precepts, and ever conduct ourselves as becomes a people redeemed by his love! May we make a proper use and improvement of the expressions of divine goodness to us in this world;

world; and then we may be affured, that we fhall be finally favoured with much higher communications of it when heaven and immortality fhall be our portion.

SERMON VIII.

On Resignation to the Will of God.

1 Sam. iii. 18.

It is the Lord; let him do what seemeth him good.

IN the present precarious state of human life, chequered and intermixed as it is with good and evil, frequent occasions may, some most certainly will, call upon us to exercise the duty exemplified in the text,—the duty of an humble acquiescence and submissive resignation to the divine dispensations.

This world, far from being so completely happy as infinite power, and perfect, absolute

absolute goodness, might have made it, was meant by its CREATOR to be a state, not of serene, undisturbed tranquillity and happiness, but of moral discipline and trial. We are born to troubles, to various disasters, which await all men in all conditions; from which neither grandeur, nor power, nor wealth, nor wisdom, nor even innocence, can give a protection. They are common to all, the greatest, the wisest, and the best. For if we look abroad into the world, where shall we find those happy sons of prosperity, whose term of years has been all white; blotted with no misfortunes, no injuries, no pains of body, or distresses of mind; no afflictions in their own person, or in the persons of others, allied to them by interest, friendship, or affection, whose sufferings they esteem their own? The law of our being, the condition of our nature, permits us not to be completely happy on this side heaven. In our present state, we may always expect vicissitudes of fortune, and that some of the numerous evils dispersed up and down the world, will meet us in our progress through it.

As resignation, then, to the divine appointments, is a duty which must sometimes, may often, be required of us, it concerns us to be acquainted with the nature of it, and to know with what sentiments and what frame of mind we should meet and receive the adverse accidents that may happen to visit us.

Let us then enquire, 1*st*, What is implied in a proper resignation to the will of Heaven; and, 2*dly*, Let us consider the rectitude and propriety of such a conduct.

I. This duty, we may observe, does not prohibit all sensibility of sufferings; it is not meant to extinguish our sensations, or reconcile us to our aversions, or to reverse the nature of things, or change our opinions about them. We are not required to divest ourselves of our feelings, and new-model the heart. A stoical insensibility of afflictive events, is what the mind, in its right state, is incapable of; nor can any religious considerations call off the attention

tention we necessarily give to what is painful and afflicting. And indeed Religion, which bids us feel for the unhappy, and weep with them that weep; which approves each softer movement of the soul, and applauds us for being touched with the distresses of others; cannot be supposed to condemn the concern we must feel for our own. Even the SAVIOUR of the world had so exquisite a sense of suffering, that, as himself said, his soul was exceeding sorrowful, even unto death; and the apprehensions of them extorted from him repeated petitions to his FATHER, that, if it were possible, the cup might pass from him.

We need not, then, think ourselves culpable, or wanting in our submission to Heaven, if a too tender sensibility should happen to betray us into some weakness and disorders, provided we suppress all angry remonstrances, all unbecoming resentments against our MAKER, and think respectfully of his providence, and express the same reverential submission with our LORD, *Father, not my will, but thine be done.*

But

But though we cannot reconcile ourselves to sufferings, nor can the most devout reverence of GOD always teach us a contempt of them; yet duty requires us to make an oblation of our wills to him; to make all our desires and aversions yield and bend to his appointments; to submit to the sufferings we would decline, as to the corrections of a parent,—whose intentions are kind, when his discipline seems severe; to drink the bitter cup we would wish to avoid, without reproaching the hand that administers the distasteful, but salutary prescription; and to say, in the submissive language of the text, *It is the Lord, let him do what seemeth him good.*— Which leads me,

II. To consider the reasonableness and propriety of this duty of submission or resignation to the divine will. And no duty, no disposition of mind, can appear more reasonable in itself, or more reverential to the Deity, when we reflect, that we are not neglected or overlooked by our CREATOR; nor dismissed from his care,

nor

nor left in the hands of Fate or Fortune: but are under the immediate protection and guardianship of the infinitely powerful PARENT of Nature; in whose presence and under whose inspection we always live and move; and who watches over us, and over all his creatures, even the least, the lowest, the most unworthy, with a care that never slumbers. The same Infinite Almighty BEING, who framed the world, is, though to us invisible, intimately present to every part of it, and inspects and superintends the whole. Unable as we are to penetrate into the counsels of his providence; though clouds and darkness are round about him; though his judgments are like the great deep, unfathomable, and his ways past finding out; yet still we may be assured, that Nature, in all her operations, obeys his voice; and that not one event can take place without his appointment or permission.

This superintendance of the Supreme BEING is a just ground for Resignation to his appointments; especially when we consider,

...sider, that his wisdom, as well as his power, is infinite, and his goodness commensurate to both: that his all-comprehending Mind sees the nature and tendencies of all things, beholds their most distant effects and consequences, and has the whole infinite chain and succession of events at once in his view: and that he is as merciful and good, as he is wise and powerful; is the friend of his creatures; and governs them, not by arbitrary mandates, or the mere dictates of will, but by the law of kindness, the laws of wisdom, mercy, and goodness.

If, then, the world be under the government of a BEING infinitely wise and good, as the Scripture assures us it is, and Reason tells us it must be; if his care extends even to the lowest objects, and the most inconsiderable events;—all our passions and desires, our hopes and fears, our every inclination, should pay homage to his sovereign will, and submit and yield to his appointments. For though we were not able to discern any kind intention of the

DEITY

Deity in the evils with which he may occasionally visit us; though we could assign no reason for their infliction, nor apprehend any salutary effect resulting from them; though the ways of Heaven were still more intricate, and the mazes of Providence less easy to be traced, than we now apprehend them to be:—still we might with assurance confide in almighty power, conducted by infinite goodness, under the direction of unerring wisdom.

Especially when we consider, that it is impossible for our imperfect sight to discern what, upon the whole, is best. Our limited understandings can only know in part; we have but a dim prospect into futurity; and, far from penetrating into the remote issues of any one event, can at the most take in but a few links of the infinitely-extended chain. This reflection should teach us to moderate our desires, and reduce them to an acquiescence in the determinations of that unerring Wisdom, which alone can determine what is good

good or evil for us. The events which in their prefent appearance feem moft afflictive, and which we are therefore moft inclined to except out of our fubmiffion; may be, and moft certainly are, defigned, in the plan of the divine government, to be the means and inftruments of producing fome good,—the channel for conveying fome bleffing here, or hereafter, which could not otherwife be obtained. For, from the fountain of inexhauftible goodnefs, no real evils, we may be affured, can flow. Abfolute evils, evils that have no relation or tendency to good, can find no place in the works of an all-perfect BEING.

When we confider, therefore, the infinite difparity between the SOVEREIGN of the world and ourfelves; when we reflect on our own ignorance and incapacity, and how unfit thefe are to comprehend the wifdom of the CREATOR, or to penetrate into the counfels of Providence, or to form a judgment of what is moft falutary to ourfelves, and moft conducive

to

to our best interests,—what can be more reasonable than to submit to the appointments of a BEING, whose presence always surrounds, whose wisdom can always guard us, whose arm is never shortened that it cannot save, nor his goodness exhausted that it will not relieve; who always has it in his power, and in his inclination, to do better for us than we can ask or think? What more just, than to resign ourselves to his guidance, not with a reluctant, extorted compliance, but with a willing acquiescence and complacency? For his wisdom best knows our true interest, cannot fail to consult, and will most certainly accomplish it, if we ourselves do not unhappily obstruct the designs of his goodness.

Too, too often, indeed, rejecting the admonitions of Religion, and giving ear to the counsels of wayward passion, we oppose and counteract the kind intentions of the DEITY; and, instead of converting adversities into blessings by a resigned and religious deportment under them, we create them

them where they are not, and aggravate them where they are. Forgetful of the various succeffive mercies we have received, the leaft of which may be greater than the beft of us deferve, we are apt to pour out undutiful murmurs and complaints: and fo unreafonable fometimes are we, as to complain of fufferings though they are not fent by Heaven, but are of our own creating; are not the inflictions of Providence, but the effects of our own iniquity, imprudence, or indifcretion; and, fometimes, even though they are not real, but exift only in imagination, and have no being but what we ourfelves give them.

But can it ever become the thing formed to expoftulate with him that formed it? Shall creatures of an hour cenfure the conduct of Eternal Wifdom? Shall we, the loweft, as far as we know, of intellectual beings; we who fubfift upon the daily alms of our CREATOR, and owe our being and well-being, all we have and are, to his favour;—fhall we prefume to repine, or remonftrate againft the equity of his adminiftration?

to the will of God.

niftration? If the Ruler of the Univerfe, who has ever one great defign in view, which he is conftantly and uniformly carrying on,—that of the greateft, moft abfolute, and general happinefs of his creatures; if he fees certain portions of temporary affliction to be conducive to that defign, or neceffary to the completion of his plan of providence:—fhall we, who cannot enter into his councils, prefume to impeach the wifdom of them? Shall we prefume to call him to an account? Shall we dare to reproach his goodnefs, or be impatient under his difpenfations?

But, unbecoming as this impatience is, what advantage can it bring with it? what other can be its effect, than to add one evil to another, and to irritate and inflame the wounds which it cannot heal? Whereas Refignation is not only a reafonable fervice, —the undoubted duty of a creature to its Creator;—but is at the fame time a wife and merciful prefcription, defigned to mitigate our pains, to heal our forrows, and adminifter fuch relief as our cafe will admit.

admit. For the misfortunes that meet us derive their chief malignity from the inward disposition with which we receive them: it is not, strictly speaking, so much events themselves, as our sentiments and opinions about them, that render us unhappy; it is our own impatience that is the sting of affliction. To correct these opinions, and this impatience, by the considerations that religion offers; to summon all our reason, and assemble all the powers of the mind, to assist in supporting what we must bear,—is the suggestion of wisdom and prudence, as well as the dictate of religion and duty.

Let us then learn an humble acquiescence in the dispensations of Heaven: let us learn to acknowledge GOD in all our ways; to view every occurrence in the light in which Religion places it; and to attribute the evils we suffer, as well as the good things we enjoy, not only to immediate and apparent causes, but to the divine will and appointment. Let us remember, that GOD, the governor of the world,

world, rules all things with his sovereign power; that no event can take place, but by his permission; that no accident is so small or inconsiderable, as to escape his notice and direction; that none can find us unguarded by his providence; that he is too wise to mistake the happiness of his creatures,—too good not to consult it.

Whatever, then, may be our state or condition, whether prosperous or adverse, let us consider it as the appointment of Heaven. Whether we receive good or evil, let us receive it as from the hand of God; let us receive his blessings with thankfulness, his inflictions without murmuring; let us be resigned to his will, and devoted to his service; let us be all submission to his dispensations, and all obedience to his laws:—so may we have good grounds to expect, when we depart from this vale of tears, this uncertain state of probation and discipline, this chequered scene of good and evil, that we may bid adieu to suffering, and take a final leave of whatever can grieve or molest us; and may hope to afcend to thofe regions of immortal blifs; where no troubles invade, no evil can ever approach; where the voice of sorrow is never heard, where true happinefs will be found, where will be fulnefs of joy, and pleafures for evermore.

SERMON IX.

On the General Judgment.

MATTH. xxiv. 44.

Therefore be ye also ready; for in such an hour as you think not, the Son of man cometh.

THE resurrection of our blessed LORD, and his triumph over death and the grave, are to be considered as the divine ratification of the authority by which he acted, and of the truth of all his declarations. We cannot now doubt, but that, as himself declared, he will come again in the glory of his FATHER, to reward every man according as his work shall

shall be. We cannot doubt but *that God has appointed a day in which he will judge the world in righteousness, by that Man whom he has ordained; whereof he hath given assurance unto all men, in that he raised him from the dead.*

In this discourse, I shall observe, 1*st*, That our Saviour CHRIST, the Son of man, is the person constituted Judge of the world; 2*dly*, That his coming will be sudden and unexpected, in such an hour as we think not; and, *lastly*, Shall consider how much it concerns us to be always in a state of readiness and preparation for that awful event.

I. Our Saviour CHRIST the Son of man is the person who will judge the world. *The Father,* says one Evangelist, *judgeth no man, but has committed all judgment unto the Son. The Son of man,* says another, *shall come in the glory of his Father, with his angels; and then shall he reward every man according to his works.* We are informed elsewhere, that *at the end of the world, the Son of man shall sit on the throne of his glory,*

and

and before him shall be gathered all nations; and that *it is he who is ordained of God to be judge of the quick and dead.* There are many other passages in Scripture of the same import, which it is unnecessary to enumerate, all representing our Saviour CHRIST as the minister of divine justice in the final allotment of rewards and punishments.

We may observe in the before mentioned passages, and where-ever our Saviour is introduced as the person who is to judge the world, that he is generally described under the appellation of *the Son of man;* **the reason of which has been supposed to be, that** he will on that occasion appear in a human form, as when he assumed our nature and dwelt upon earth. He will in like manner, we are told, descend from heaven, as he ascended to it; but his appearance will then be with far superior majesty, and more like the Son of HIM who is Lord of Heaven and Earth.

At his first advent, when he descended from the heavenly regions, he submitted to all the humiliations and sufferings of mortality,

tality. At his second advent, the veil which had obscured his divine nature will be done away; and he will appear in the glory of his father, in a manner becoming the dignity of his high office, attended with an infinite host of angels: *Thousands of thousands shall stand before him, and ten thousand times ten thousand shall minister unto him.* He will then deck himself with light as with a garment, and will be clothed with such superior lustre, that St John, in his vision, represents all nature vanishing and disappearing amidst the refulgence of his glory. *I saw,* says he, *a great white throne, and him that sat on it, from whose face the earth and the heavens fled away, and there was no place found for them.*

Our Saviour CHRIST is, then, the person constituted Judge of the world. And it ought to be considered as a clear explicit declaration of our MAKER's compassionate intentions, that the same Person is to sit in judgment, who in mercy condescended to assume our nature and dwell among us. For what more equitable or
fa-

favourable judge could even our wishes figure to us, than the very perfon who offered himfelf a voluntary facrifice to redeem and fave loft mankind? than he who for our fake quitted the heavenly throne, and became fubject to our infirmities? As our nature was thus highly favoured by him, may we not humbly hope, that mercy will prevail againft judgement, and that forgivenefs will be refufed to none but fuch as have rendered themfelves utterly unworthy of it?

II. The coming of our LORD will be fudden and unexpected, in fuch an hour as we think not. *The day of the Lord will come*, fay the Scriptures, *as a thief in the night*. In the laft age of the world, its diffolution will be an event as much unexpected, as, in the days of Noah, was the deluge which covered the face of the earth. Whilft mankind are engaged in their different purfuits; whilft fome are purchafing pleafure at the expence of every virtue, others attempting to extend their power by every method of oppreffion, and almoft moſt all as attentive to the concerns of the world, as if thoſe concerns were to ſubſiſt for ever;—they will ſee an unexpected, but laſting, period put to all their pur‐ ſuits,—and all their hopes and projects loſt in the general devaſtation. Whilſt ſome are perhaps mocking at this awful predic‐ tion of our LORD, and ſaying, Where is the promiſe of his coming? they will be ſurpriſed with the ſudden and amazing proof of its completion.

For the ſcriptures do not inform us, that any preparatory notice will be given of this final revolution. There will be no uncommon appearances in the heavens or the earth to preſignify its approach; no viſible decay in the conſtitution of Na‐ ture, no prognoſtics of its diſſolution, no apparent ſymptoms of diſorder. The ſun will continue, as uſual, to rule the day, and the moon to govern the night. The ſeaſons will move on in their appointed round, the earth produce its annual ſtores, and the world ſeem likely to ſubſiſt for a long ſucceſſion of ages. Nature, how‐
ever,

ever, notwithstanding these appearances of health and vigour, will on a sudden sicken and expire in violent convulsions.

But of that day and hour, says our blessed SAVIOUR, knoweth no man, no not the angels which are in heaven, neither the SON, but the FATHER. Over that event GOD has thrown a thick veil, through which no eye but his own can penetrate. But of this we may be assured, that he is equally benevolent and merciful in whatever he reveals, and whatever he withholds from us. As he is kind in imparting to us the knowledge of such things as are necessary or useful to be known, he is no less merciful in concealing others which might be hurtful. He hath informed us of whatever is necessary to prompt and animate us to assiduity and vigilance in our duty; but hath withheld that knowledge which might tempt and betray us into a slothful and careless confidence.

If the day and hour of the last judgement were known with precision and certainty;

tainty; its terrors, if near, would intimidate too much; if diftant, might affect us too little: in the former cafe, we fhould be too neglectful of our affairs in this world; in the latter, too inattentive to the concerns of the next. GOD, therefore, in all the difpenfations of his providence equally wife and good, and who defires to have both our hopes and our fears, our knowledge and our ignorance, to be alike inftrumental to our happinefs, has been pleafed to hide the important fecret in his own bofom; to conceal from us the period of the general judgment, in order that we may be always prepared, without being terrified; attentive always to our falvation in the next world, without too much indifference to the concerns of the prefent.—Which leads me,

III. and *laftly*, To confider the wifdom of holding ourfelves always in a ftate of preparation for the coming of our LORD. Whenever we reflect, that the prefent life is meant to be introductory to another, infinitely more important ftate of being, and

and that the awful period is approaching, how soon we know not, when we muſt all appear before the tribunal of the righteous Sovereign of the earth, whoſe irreverſible ſentence will be deciſive of our fate for ever;—this ſurely ought to create in us a moſt ſerious ſolicitude to avoid every behaviour that may offend our Almighty Judge, and apply to every duty and virtue that can recommend us to his approbation and acceptance.

It is matter of juſt ſurpriſe, that many who profeſs their conviction of a future judgment, ſhould be as inattentive to that great event, and appear to live as little under its influence, as others who have no ſuch expectations: a conduct highly reproachful to human reaſon. The loweſt degree of probability for an event of ſuch conſequence, ought, doubtleſs, to demand attention, and excite us to a preparation for it. But when we have ſufficient and ſatisfactory evidence,—ſuch evidence as leaves in the mind no diffidence or ſuſpicion of its certainty;—ſurely, if we would act in any degree as becomes rational beings, we ought to make it the object of serious and frequent meditation; and be above all things concerned, by a strict attention to every duty, to entitle ourselves to a favourable sentence from the heavenly throne. This should seem the natural effect of our belief of a future judgment.

And to impress us with a more serious and awful sense of that solemnity, and to animate us to the most vigilant preparation for it,—the coming of our LORD, for that purpose, is described with all the striking circumstances of pomp, magnificence, and majesty, that seem likely to affect the mind. He will come, we are informed, in his own glory, and his Father's, with all the holy angels. At his appearance the face of nature will be changed, and the frame of the world dissolved. The heavens shall pass away with a great noise; the elements shall melt with fervent heat; the earth also, and the works that are therein, shall be burnt up. The representation which the Scripture draws of this awful scene, is

meant

meant to animate us to a due preparation for it; and, seeing all these things are to be dissolved, to excite us to consider well what manner of persons we ought to be in all holy conversation and godliness.

At what distance this great event **may** be, or how long our LORD may delay his coming, we are not informed. **Our LORD** himself has foretold, that *as a snare it will come upon all them that dwell on the face of the whole earth*, and will surprise them in **such** an hour as they think not. The judgment of the great day may possibly, even now, be near approaching; in which case, if we are unprepared, it will be too late for preparation to begin. Such as our condition is, such will be our irreversible fate for endless ages. If we **are not in** readiness, the opportunity for it, and **we** ourselves, **are** for ever lost.

It may indeed be supposed, with more probability, that this may be a remote event, and that the general judgment may be at the distance of many ages; but yet **another** awful event must soon and certainly

tainly happen. The period when our state of probation will determine, and our trial be concluded, cannot be far distant: and that event is, in effect, with regard to our future condition, the same as that of Judgement; and, like it too, unknown and wrapt in darkness. For such is the natural weakness of the human frame; such the various disorders and unknown accidents to which we stand exposed; so numerous, so unseen, the avenues to eternity; that we ought not, cannot, be secure even of to-morrow.

Shall we, then, with an imprudence which we cannot but disapprove, shall we risk all our future hopes; shall we postpone the care of the soul to some supposed hereafter, or even to to-morrow, when we know not what events a day may bring forth?

We are often tempted, indeed, to indulge the pleasing visionary prospect of a long succession of years, especially if we are favoured with the appearances of health and strength. Our attachment to life and self-

self-partiality are apt to perfuade us, that we shall live long and fee good days; that our term of years may be prolonged to the utmost period; that a gradual decay of constitution will give us timely **notice** to prepare for hereafter; and on that **pre-**sumption, we lay aside or postpone all attention to futurity.

But the hope of long life is but the **insi-**nuation of self-flattery. We should consider, that others have been favoured with the same salutary appearances, have indulged the same hopes; that these hopes and appearances have deceived them, and may equally deceive us. How many must we have known, who, amidst all the apparent symptoms, and the most flattering promises, of long life, and amidst all the confidence of presumed security, have **been** unexpectedly taken captive by the universal conqueror, who putteth all things under his feet?

If, then, Heaven has not vouchfafed to certify us how long we **have** to live; has not informed us of our **end,** and of the number of our days;—it is surely wisdom to make it our serious and habitual, as it is undoubtedly our most important, concern, to be prepared always to give obedience to the heavenly voice, whenever it shall please the Lord of life and death to summon us to his tribunal.

It is not here to be understood, that a future judgment should be the perpetual object of our meditations, or that we should be always directly and formally preparing for it; for that is incompatible with the state and condition of human life, and with the duties we owe to the world and to ourselves. But in order to be habitually prepared, let us begin an immediate reformation of what we find amiss in our manners, and live in a regular persevering obedience to the divine laws. The best, the only secure preparative for hereafter, are the virtues of a good life. Without these, the last hour may, when we look not for it, hurry us away to judgement before our accounts are ready, and
convey

convey us out of this world before we have made provision for the next.

Every instance that occurs of sudden mortality, seems to admonish us in the language of the text, *Be ye also ready; for in such an hour as ye think not, the Son of man cometh.* Dreadful indeed will be the terrors of that hour to the unprepared servant, when surprised by his LORD; but blessed the condition of those whom he shall find vigilant in the duties of his service, and employed in pious efforts to merit his favour. To such, welcome will be the tidings that the LORD is at hand; and happier far than the day of their birth, will be that of death. May we resolve to seize and improve the present opportunities of life, that we may be prepared for that awful event which is approaching, and may in consequence inherit the blessedness of those servants whom their LORD, when he cometh, shall find watching!

SERMON X.

On Public Worship.

Preached at opening the New Episcopal Chapel in Edinburgh, on Sunday, October 9. 1774.

An OCCASIONAL PRAYER.

O THOU Supreme Almighty BEING, whose goodness is everlasting, whose providential care extends to all thy creatures, look down from the habitation of thy holiness, upon us thy servants, who are here assembled to present our supplications before thee.

We

We at this time particularly implore thy acceptance of the adorations which shall be offered in this House of Prayer, which we now dedicate and appropriate to thy service. Vouchsafe to accept this our offering, and to regard with an eye of mercy the supplicants who here approach thy presence.

Let the influence of thy Holy Spirit accompany the religious instructions and exhortations which shall here be delivered, that we may both perceive and know what things we ought to do, and also may have grace and power faithfully to fulfil the same. But if we sin against thee, as there is no man that liveth and sinneth not; yet if we repent, and make our supplications unto thee in this house, and return unto thee

thee with all our heart, and with all our soul, then hear thou from heaven thy dwelling-place, and forgive us our transgressions wherein we have transgressed against thee. And this we beg for JESUS CHRIST his sake; in whose holy name and words we further address thee----- 'Our FATHER which art in heaven,' &c.

PSAL. XCV. 6.

O come, let us worship, and fall down, and kneel before the Lord our maker.

ON this first occasion of assembling within these walls, now sacred to Religion, the homage which we here assemble to pay to the adorable AUTHOR of our

our being, should seem a proper subject for our meditation. For which reason, I have selected the words of the text, taken from an hymn supposed to have been an introductory part of divine service in the Jewish Temple, and for the same purpose adopted by our Church.

In discoursing on which, I shall consider, 1*st*, Our obligations to worship the LORD our MAKER; and, 2*dly*, The religious effects consequent on a due observance of this duty.

I. That GOD ought to be worshipped, is a principle of natural religion, immediately arising from an acknowledgment of his existence, in whatever relation we consider him. For, is he our Maker, the Father of the whole family of mankind? he has then a parental right to every expression of filial respect and reverence. Is he the LORD, the Sovereign of nature, whose dominion extends to the ends of the earth, and to the utmost limits of creation, if creation be indeed limited? he has then a just claim to universal homage, and his authority ought to be acknowledged and revered by us and all his subjects and dependents. Does he, as Ruler of the world, by a powerful, though invisible hand, conduct all the operations of nature? and is our existence, and our whole happiness, dependent on his will? we must then think it reasonable to present our petitions, and address him for protection and favour. Is he our Supreme Benefactor, to whose unsolicited goodness we owe our being, and every provision made for our well-being; who has been liberal in his favours, and every day confers some new, or repeats some former blessing? our gratitude must then acknowledge our obligations to offer up our praises and adorations for his goodness, and for the wonders he doth for the children of men. Is he the most amiable of all Beings, in whom all possible and conceivable perfections centre, the Parent of good, the Source of all created excellence? he is then worthy of our best affections, and every sentiment of our heart must pay homage to him.

These

These perfections have a natural **claim** to love and veneration, to **all** the tribute of praise, and to much more than the poor pittance of honour that we can pay **to the** Sovereign, the Parent, and Guardian of creation. Are respect and deference paid even to our fellow **men of superior** dignity and **character?** **as much as** the Supreme, **clothed with** majesty **and honour, surpasses all other** beings, so much higher title has HE to our **reverence and** veneration. **Are the** expressions of a grateful heart due to inferior benefactors? as far as the blessings derived from HIM, the Fountain of all **blessings, exceed the** good offices we receive one from another, **so** much better right has HE **to our gratitude and praise.**

But the duty I am now considering, **requires** not the aid of any **train of** reasoning to recommend **and approve it** to the calmest judgment of the mind. **No argument** can render it clearer than **it appears** by its own light. That **we ought to worship** the Lord our Maker, by the best expressions

pressions of regard, submission, veneration, and devotion, is as self-evident as the obligation to any of the social duties. We have an intuitive perception of the propriety and rectitude of walking humbly with our GOD, as well as of doing justly or shewing mercy to men. Reason, or the moral principle in us, with a voice and in a language hardly to be misunderstood, dictates this duty.

And here we may observe, that to the duty of Prayer, a principal part of divine worship, our CREATOR seems to have added a supplemental direction. There is impressed on the human mind an instinctive determination, a natural propensity to Prayer, which, on sudden emergencies, acts instantaneously, without waiting the issue of the slower councils of Reason. On many occasions, in seasons of affliction particularly, the heart moves spontaneously towards GOD; and by a mere natural impulse, without deliberation, we look up to him for protection, and pour out our fears and dangers to him.

This

This inftinctive direction of the mind, not given in vain, fhould feem an indication that we are formed for piety and devotion; from which we cannot depart, without deviating from the line of duty which nature points out. No man, perhaps, could ever totally fupprefs in himfelf this propenfion in feafons of fevere diftrefs, or at the hour of approaching death. At that awful hour, the Atheift no longer finds confolation in the laboured refinements of philofophy, no longer leans on the broken reed of abftrufe fpeculation; but adopts the fentiments of nature, lifts up his heart to Heaven in fecret fupplications, and recommends his foul to the great SUPPORTER of his exiftence.

But not only the impulfe we feel on fome emergencies, but the univerfal voice of mankind, fpeaks the fenfe of nature in this particular. The feveral nations in the world, however differing in their cuftoms, manners, and characters, have in all ages been united in the opinion of an adoration due to their CREATOR. Into whatever

whatever regions we caſt our eyes, we meet with religious ceremonies, altars, temples, or places ſacred to a Deity; among every people we diſcover a reverence of a Supreme Being. If we look back into the remoteſt ages of antiquity, we find, that, even in the infancy of the world, men began to call upon the name of the LORD. Noah, we read, and Abraham, and Iſaac, erected altars, without any divine injunction, ſo far as we are informed. The Pagan nations, amidſt all their ignorance and darkneſs, adopted ſome rites of religious worſhip. If you ſearch the world, ſays an eminent heathen author*, you may find cities without wealth, without walls, without princes: but no man ever ſaw a city without a deity, without a temple, and without prayers. Whence it ſhould ſeem, that devotion is natural to the human mind, as univerſal as the belief of a Supreme Being, and as characteriſtic of our ſpecies as reaſon itſelf.

Need

---

* Plutarch.

Need I further to obferve, that the duty of divine worfhip is not only required by the law of reafon and nature, but that the Chriftian LAWGIVER has added his authority to the natural obligations we were under, and has enjoined his followers to offer up their fupplications to the throne of GOD, not only in private addreffes, but in focial and public folemnities, and has promifed his prefence in our religious affemblies; and has added alfo an inftruction not given in nature, That we fhould offer up our prayers in HIS name.

II. The worfhip of GOD is attended with the happieft effects. It is itfelf virtue, and inftrumental to virtue. It is to be confidered, not only as a fingle act of duty, but as introductory to every other duty, and the beft means of forming the mind to univerfal rectitude and goodnefs. Divine worfhip has a natural tendency to fet GOD always before us; to bring us under an awful fenfe of his infpection; and by reminding us of the immediate prefence of that BEING who is of purer

eyes

eyes than to behold iniquity, must, if we are at all susceptive of religious impressions, check every inclination to vice, and animate us to every virtue. No other method can be conceived more effectual to keep alive in the soul a sense of God's superintendent providence, and of our dependent state; to familiarize ideas of duty; to open the mind to serious reflections, devout sentiments, and virtuous principles.

We may with truth assert, that if men were more regular in their attendance on the duties of devotion, the sentiments thus frequently infused into the mind could scarce fail to give a moral tincture to their manners. They would be more submissive and resigned to the will of Heaven, more just and benevolent to men, more indifferent to the seducements of the world; their passions more temperate, their whole conduct more correct. Devout intercourse with God would in some measure gradually assimilate them to the Divine

vine Nature, and render them holy as HE is holy.

Public worship, we may also observe, may naturally be expected to be promotive of peace and good-will. When we here assemble in the duties of devotion, we ought all to consider ourselves as allied to each other, as brethren, heirs of the same hopes, children of the same FATHER who is in heaven. Here, therefore, every malevolent, every unfriendly passion, should subside. When we here see the circle of our brethren and fellow-supplicants all paying their joint homage and adoration at the throne of grace; all addressing the mercy of our general FATHER, in supplications for each other, and for our common salvation; and all aspiring to those mansions of peace and love, where we shall, we hope, for ever associate;—let this prospect, this scene of piety, which now presents itself to view; this image, such as earth can afford, of heaven, let it unite us here, as there, in the bonds of affection, that we may happily, as brethren, dwell

dwell together in unanimity, harmony, and benevolence.

It may appear, then, that religious worship has a powerful tendency to imprefs an habitual fenfe of GOD's prefence and providence, and to plant and cultivate various virtues and moral affections in the foul. Hence the utility of public, ftated forms of religion, which are the evident means of preferving in the world, fo far as it is preferved, a public fenfe of morality and duty. Were no public fervices of religion obferved, and no times or places appropriated to that purpofe, men would be lefs attentive to the duties they owe to GOD and to each other; and would be fo abforbed by the diffipations or cares of the world, that they would pay little regard to that care which is moft needful, the care of their falvation. Mankind in general, formed more for active than contemplative life, find fo little leifure or inclination for reflection, that public and frequent memorials of their dependence upon GOD are neceffary to preferve in
their

their minds an habitual remembrance of their CREATOR, and of the duty they owe him. For if inattention to the DEITY, and an indifference to piety and virtue, be the subjects of general complaint, even now amidst all the opportunities of regular, social worship; may it not be presumed, that, without those monitions, men would be much more forgetful of their religious obligations, and that a long train of immoral and fatal consequences would ensue?

But this point need not be farther insisted on: it is admitted even by the adversaries of religion and public worship, when they assert them to be only state-engines, or political institutions, devised by legislators to awe mankind into an observance of those duties which are essential to public peace and their common interests. This assertion is an argument in favour of the doctrine it would oppose: for if religion and social worship be necessary and essential, or even conducive, to the public happiness; certain it is, they must have the approbation, and be worthy of the injunction of that BEING, whose object, in all his dispensations, is the happiness of his creatures.

I have hitherto considered the duty of divine worship in general, without pointing out the peculiar excellence of that mode of worship, of which your attendance in this place speaks your approbation. But as this may seem unnecessary, permit me rather to observe, in what high estimation we ought to hold the favour of Providence, in assigning our lot in a land, happy in a constitution, and a system of laws, the most favourable in the world to the rights of human nature; where we are permitted, in religious matters, to dissent from public establishment; where the principles of toleration are understood, and acknowledged; where the invaluable blessings of religious liberty are enjoyed to an extent not known to other nations, nor till of late possessed by our own. Nature, or rather its AUTHOR, never meant to establish an uniformity of opinions.

nions. He has not given to all men the same intellectual discernment, nor placed us all in the same commodious situation for the discovery of truth: religious objects, consequently, must be observed from different points of view, and appear in different lights and positions. A diversity of sentiments is evidently the plan of nature; and is not to be considered as an evil, except when we render it such by discordant passions.

But very different from the genius and characteristic virtue of our religion is every degree of discord on account of such diversity. Would we evince the superior excellence of the doctrines and devotional rites of our church? let us attempt it by the best of arguments,—by appealing to their moral effects, their superior influence on our lives and manners. *Let the tree*, according to our SAVIOUR's expression, *be known by its fruit*. By this we may best estimate its value. This will be our best vindication. By such arguments we may, we ought, earnestly, too earnestly we cannot, contend for the honour of our holy profeſſion. Religious altercations have ſeldom been deciſive, or produced any other conviction, than that, **where** opinions differ, affections are apt to be at variance; and that the true ſpirit of religion is often loſt amidſt the contentions about it.

But to return from this digreſſion: If it appears, that divine worſhip is both a primary and an inſtrumental duty of our religion; if it naturally reminds us of what we often forget, our dependence upon God for all we have and all we are, for every preſent enjoyment, and all our future hopes; if it tends to cultivate in us, what we too much neglect, a benevolence of heart, and a diſpoſition to every virtue; —it highly concerns us, not to be wanting to ourſelves in a duty which is itſelf a reaſonable ſervice, of intrinſic obligation and rectitude, and comes further recommended by the happieſt influence on our minds and manners.

To God, then, the Sovereign of Nature, the Greateſt, Wiſeſt, Beſt of Beings,

be

be it our care to pay our frequent homage. It is the duty he requires, and we are under every obligation to pay. But let us remember, when we approach him in the duties of his fervice, that we muſt worſhip him in the beſt manner we can; and the beſt will fall infinitely ſhort of what is due to his perfections. We muſt worſhip him in ſpirit and in truth, with the underſtanding, and with the heart. In vain ſhould we approach him with forms and appearances, or with the moſt humiliating attitudes, unaccompanied with internal reverence; in vain ſhould we fall down and kneel before the LORD our Maker, unleſs we at the ſame time humble and proſtrate the mind.

For this ſolemn duty let us always prepare ourſelves, by previouſly impreſſing on the mind the moſt reſpectful ideas of that infinite BEING whom we here addreſs; and during our attendance on his ſervice, let us retain an awful ſenſe of the majeſty of his preſence. As often as we here aſſemble, to preſent ourſelves before the

Most High God, let us leave, as much as may be, the world and its concernments, all ideas of its cares or pleasures, behind us: let us, on the wings of holy Contemplation, elevate our hearts to heaven; nor let us suffer them, till we depart hence, to descend to the things of the earth.

Permit me further to observe, that when we return from the duties of this holy assembly, we are still to retain the religious impressions which we have here received: we are not to retire from God: we are still to hold a sacred intercourse, by an attention to him in our whole conduct; by acknowledging him in all our ways; by considering his will as our invariable guide, his providence the object of our dependence, his favour the aim of our ambition; and by rendering him continual homage in the uniform obedience of a good life.

To this good end, this obedience, and the felicity consequent upon it, may this House of Prayer now erected prove happily subservient; may it be the means, under Providence, of recommending and promoting

moting rational piety; of reclaiming the sinner, and confirming the just; of elucidating the doctrines, and enforcing the duties, of the Christian system; and of exhibiting a just portrait of religion: which, to be esteemed, requires only to be fairly represented; and when viewed in its native form and features, adorned with every moral grace and virtue, and not dishonoured with the garb of superstition or enthusiasm, must to every intellectual eye appear in perfect beauty,—the object of universal veneration.

May that supreme, all-propitious Being, to whose service this our temple is dedicated, and without the light of whose countenance their labour is but lost that built it; may he vouchsafe to favour the pious hopes of its founders, and to prosper this work of our hands upon us, by shedding down his blessings, and imparting to every faithful worshipper within these walls, the effectual, though imperceptible influence of his Grace. May the seed of true religion, here sown, as in good ground, spring up,—and, watered with the dew of heaven, be abundantly productive of the fruits of the Spirit, love, peace, gentleness, meekness, and every virtue. And may we co-operate with the secret influence. May our lives be as pure, as our religion is holy. May the piety of the supplicants be the principal decoration of this structure. May the beauty of holiness appear equally in our manners and in the conduct of our devotions. May we here find the way that leadeth to everlasting life. And may this, which is now none other than the house of GOD, be to all of us the gate of Heaven.

SERMON XI.

Internal Excellence of the GOSPEL.

PHIL. iii. 8.

I count all things but loss, for the excellency of the knowledge of Christ Jesus my Lord.

THE peculiar excellence of the Christian doctrine, and its conformity to the dictates of the best and most improved reason, is one argument of its divine original, without which all external evidence would be defective and insufficient. It is indeed the privilege of the gospel to come recommended to us by various concurring attestations of its divine authority; to be supported by every evidence that the nature

ture of revelation will admit; and to be no less eminently confirmed and distinguished by the intrinsic excellence of its doctrines and precepts, than by the exterior evidence of miracles and prophesies.

My present design is, to shew, that the Christian doctrine is worthy of that God from whose mercies to mankind it claims its high original; and to illustrate its peculiar excellence, in the following particulars, viz. as it exhibits the most just representation of the nature of the DEITY, prescribes the most rational worship, presents to us the purest and most perfect moral precepts, and proposes the most effectual motives to the practice of universal virtue and goodness: for in these particulars must consist the principal excellence of any religious system.

I. The excellence of that doctrine which the SON of GOD published to the world, may appear from its just descriptions of the divine nature. For the gospel informs us, that GOD is infinite in all perfections, all-sufficient, self-subsistent, almighty, omnipresent,

present, and eternal: that he is a pure Spirit,—an opinion not generally received in the Heathen world; and to be worshipped in spirit and in truth,—a doctrine unknown to, or unobserved by, the Jews. He is represented as the only true GOD; infinite in majesty, unlimited in his essence, unsearchable in his providence, incomprehensible to his creatures; too high for our speculations, too exalted for description; infinitely great and excellent, beyond whatever our conceptions can form; filling heaven and earth with his presence; including all space, and contained in none.

He is described to have been from everlasting, infinitely happy in himself, and the inexhaustible fountain of universal and endless happiness to his creatures. His power is set forth, in that he is said to be LORD of heaven and earth; that with him all things are possible; that he has heaven for his throne, and earth for his footstool; and that angels and archangels, and all the company of heaven, are the servants that do his pleasure: that his power

power created all things; that his providence fuſtaineth all things; and that univerſal nature is obedient to his word. The Scriptures repreſent him as infinitely elevated above the higheſt of his creatures, but not neglecting or deſpiſing the meaneſt; far exalted above all bleſſing and praiſe, yet accepting our moſt imperfect prayers and praiſes, when offered with a faithful and upright heart. There alſo his peculiar care, his paternal concern, for us his children, is abundantly diſplayed; foraſmuch as the very hairs of our head are ſaid to be all numbered. His compaſſion to ſinners appears in his ſending his SON into the world to call them to repentance. He is not repreſented ſevere, cruel, and vindictive, the object of awful terror; to be appeaſed therefore with human ſacrifices, like the gods of the Heathen; but as the FATHER of mercies, the GOD of peace and love, and of all conſolation.

Whence it may appear, that the repreſentation or portrait of the Divine Nature, as exhibited in the Scripture, far from being

ing difcordant with our natural notions of the DEITY, is fuch as reafon muft immediately approve, and admit to be in every refpect worthy of his Supreme perfection.

II. The next inquiry is, Whether the worfhip inftituted in the gofpel, and required to be paid, is fuch as is worthy to be received? And here many excellent things may be defervedly fpoken of the Chriftian inftitution. For the worfhip of the heart, not of the lip, is what CHRIST every where enjoins. He requires us to adore our MAKER in the fecret recefles of our foul; not to pray ftanding in the corners of the ftreets with oftentatious pride, but to breathe out the fervour of our heart in privacy and retirement; to enter into our clofet, and let our devotions filently afcend to HIM who feeth in fecret. The fincerity of the heart, the purity of the mind, the fervour of our affections, productive of genuine goodnefs, is the incenfe which we are inftructed to offer up to Heaven. To worfhip GOD in humility;

mility; to approach him with reverence; not to trust in our own righteousness, but in his manifold and great mercies; to acknowledge and bewail our own sinfulness; to suppress an opinion of religious merit; to disclaim all worthiness on our part, and with awful adoration to implore the mercies of a gracious CREATOR,——is the spiritual and rational worship of the Gospel.

If, then, sincerity of heart, and humility of mind, become the supplicant; if GOD ought to be worshipped in spirit and in truth, not with mere bodily service; if a pious fervour is a fit property of our addresses to the throne of grace; if to prostrate ourselves before GOD with all our heart, with all our soul, and with all our mind, be the reasonable duty of a creature to his CREATOR; then the Christian doctrine, with respect to the nature or mode of religious worship, is such as may be justly deemed of GOD.

III. But further, the Christian institution teaches and enjoins the purest Morality.

lity. It comprises all the best precepts and rules of life which had been delivered by the wisest of the ancient philosophers; but improved and refined, as it were, to the highest purity, and unmingled with the superstitious and absurd opinions which had adulterated and debased their systems.

The most spotless purity, the most immaculate holiness, is the rule of our actions, and the measure of our duty. Thus we are commanded to be perfect, as our FATHER which is in heaven is perfect. To this purpose is that divine sermon on the mount; wherein is contained the most sublime virtue which Heaven could prescribe, or man can practise: not an exterior, formal sanctity; but a sincere, unfeigned purity of heart, constant and faithful to his duty. Hence it is, that not the commission only, but even the intention or conception, of guilt is criminal. The source and spring of our actions, the heart, is hereby secured. So pure, so spiritual, is the genius of our religion!

It

It in a particular manner recommends the virtue of charity, or benevolence; which, according to the plan of the gospel, ought to be the leading principle, the animating spirit of every Christian society, disposing all men to perform the duties and kind offices they owe to one another. Christianity is the most charitable, benevolent institution in the world; one proof, among others, that it is derived from the Best and most Benevolent of Beings. All malignity and revenge are wholly forbidden; and the most extensive love, the most diffusive benevolence, is required: benevolence not restricted to the narrow limits of a party, sect, or nation; but extending itself over the face of the whole earth, even to our enemies. No difference in opinions, no diversity of interests, not even injurious treatment, must extinguish Christian charity. Nor is it this single virtue which we stand engaged to perform: but *whatsoever things are lovely, whatsoever things are pure, honest, just, and of good report*, these we are to practise; not from vanity

vanity or oftentation, not to receive praife of men, but from fentiments of duty, and a principle of obedience to GOD. *All things whatfoever we would that men fhould do unto us, even fo we muſt do unto them;* and the **leaſt** commandment muſt not be broken.

Such is the lovely form, fuch the amiable fpirit **of the** Chriſtian inſtitution; fuch its **benevolent** principles; fuch the **rational duties it** enjoins. No religion **ever** prefcribed better rules of conduct; none differing **from it** can be fo good. It is not in the **power of** human underſtanding to devife a **fyftem of** duties more confonant to our natural **notions** of GOD, or **more conducive to the** happinefs and wellbeing of Man. And this alone may fuggeſt **to us its** divine original; for a religion which **enjoins no** other duties but fuch **as are conformable to** the eternal laws of GOD and nature, and whofe fole aim and tendency is **to** promote univerfal goodnefs and virtue and happinefs, muſt either be immediately derived from GOD,

or

or at least must be agreeable to him, and worthy of him.

IV. Lastly, the Gospel presents the most powerful motives of future retribution, in order to invite or compel us, as far as free agents can be compelled, to the observance and practice of religion and virtue. Virtue may be amiable, worthy to be chosen, fit to be practised, at all times, by all rational beings; its ways may be ways of pleasantness, and all its paths chiefly lead to peace. But yet, since vice has likewise its pleasures, the world its allurements, and we walk in the midst of temptations that are always offering to corrupt and seduce, it is fit that rewards and punishments should be annexed to the obedience required: not that the thing formed has any right to claim reward, or withhold obedience from him that formed it; but the wisdom of a lawgiver best consults the honour and authority of his laws by such sanctions as most effectually operate in securing obedience.

Hope and fear are the great springs of human

human actions; and nothing can take faster hold of our nature than the hope of everlasting happiness, or the fears of future punishment. These are the most powerful and effectual enforcements of obedience that can possibly be offered to mankind. To angels, or beings of superior rank, sense of duty may be an adequate and sufficient motive of action: but man, frail and corrupt, will have respect to the recompence of reward; for which reason, life and immortality were brought to light by the gospel.

In the dark, benighted ages of Heathen ignorance, before the SUN of Righteousness arose, and his light shone upon the world, mankind might entertain suspicions and doubts concerning a future existence; they knew not, when they descended into the grave, whither it would convey them, or whether it might not put a period to their being. But now we know, that we shall rise again, and give an account of our works. Now we may with alacrity enter into the ways of holiness, and with unwearied perseverance run the race that is set before us; since the righteous, we are assured, will obtain the prize of life eternal; and death, the terror of our nature, will be to the righteous an introduction to heaven, and will open to them the gate of everlasting bliss.

If, then, rewards and punishments are the proper sanctions of the divine laws; if their authority is thereby best preserved sacred and inviolate;—the doctrine which the world's Redeemer taught is worthy of GOD, forasmuch as it proposes and enforces the most powerful and effectual considerations to encourage and animate us to virtue, and to dissuade and deter from vice. If, then, our religion comes recommended to us by various concurring proofs of its authority; if its external evidences are confirmed and supported by the internal characters of its truth,—by the rectitude, purity, and excellence, of its doctrines and duties;—then we have the fullest confirmation of its divine original, that the nature of revelation will admit;

then

then may we be assured, that GOD hath spoken unto us by his SON; and then ought we also to consider well the necessity of conforming our lives to the rules of the gospel, of letting our manners be as pure as our religion is holy, of walking worthy of the vocation wherewith we are called, and of letting our conversation be as becometh the gospel of CHRIST.

SERMON XII.

ASCENSION.

ACTS i. 9.

And when he had spoken these things, while they beheld, he was taken up, and a cloud received him out of their sight.

AS every circumstance relative to the redemption of mankind is a proper object of a Christian's meditations, solemn seasons have been therefore set apart for the commemoration of our blessed SAVIOUR's incarnation, passion, and resurrection.

What I shall consider at present is his ascension into heaven; and shall observe, 1*st*, The circumstances of our LORD's ascension;

scension; and, 2*dly*, The evidences we have of its truth.

I. Our blessed LORD, we are informed, after his resurrection, showed himself alive to his disciples by many infallible proofs; admitting them to familiar converse; allowing them to handle him, that they might be sure they were not deceived by any illusive appearance; illuminating their understandings; explaining to them subjects, of which, before his death, he had given general intimations; expounding to them, out of the prophets, the things concerning himself, and pertaining to the kingdom of GOD; and promising to be with them, **by the influence of his Spirit, always, even unto the end.** Our SAVIOUR, we read, was seen by his disciples, after his resurrection, for the space of forty days. But whether, during this interval between his resurrection and final ascension, he continued constantly upon earth with his disciples and followers, or whether he ascended on the morning of the resurrection, and afterwards appeared only

only occafionally, as often as their conviction or inftruction might require, has been matter of doubt.

But however this was, when our bleffed LORD had fufficiently inftructed his difciples, he afcended finally from them, and was received up into heaven; was conveyed from earth to the higheft ftate of glory, and the moft immediate prefence of the DEITY. For though the Divine BEING is every-where equally prefent; tho' he fills all fpace, and inhabits immenfity; and cannot, ftrictly fpeaking, exift effentially in one place more than in another; —yet the heavenly region, where he has thought fit to unveil his glory, and manifeft his prefence in the moft confpicuous manner, and which he has appointed to be the refidence of numberlefs hofts of angels, the fervants that do his pleafure, is in Scripture faid to be his throne and his habitation; and thither it was that our bleffed LORD afcended. And though there may be different regions of happinefs, fuited to the various orders of fpiritual

ritual beings (as St Paul's being caught up to the third heaven should seem to imply); yet since our SAVIOUR is said to be gone into the holy place, even heaven itself, to appear before the presence of GOD, to have been made higher than the angels, and to have ascended far above the heavens, there is good reason to understand heaven in the text, in the most exalted sense of the word, as the seat of supreme felicity, and the most conspicuous and august residence of the Divine Glory.

The ascension of the MESSIAH was, we may observe, prefigured under the Jewish dispensation. According to the **author of** the epistle to the Hebrews, the high-priest's entrance into the holy of holies, the innermost and most sacred part of the **temple,** performed once a year, on the solemn day of atonement, did presignify, that CHRIST, the MESSIAH, should once suffer death, as a propitiation for the sins of mankind, and after that ascend into the Heaven of heavens. The Jews believed, that the tabernacle

nacle was meant to reprefent this world, and the holy of holies to typify the higheft heaven. Wherefore, as the high-prieft did once in the year offer a facrifice for the fins of the people, and with the blood thereof enter into the holy of holies; fo the MESSIAH was, by the one oblation of himfelf once offered, to enter into the holy place, not made with hands, eternal in the heavens; and there to prefent the facrifice he offered, and his blood that was fhed, for the fins of the world.

II. I proceed to obferve the evidence we have of the truth of our LORD's afcenfion.

Though it is not poffible we fhould acquire the fame certainty of this fact, as thofe whofe fenfes informed them of its truth (the moft unexceptionable tradition or teftimony being undoubtedly weaker than the evidence of fenfe); yet if we have now all the evidence that any remote fact is capable of, and fuch evidence as never fails to command affent in other cafes, reafon will require our affent alfo in this.

If, then, it appears that the witneffes of our

our LORD's ascension were persons of unquestionable integrity and understanding; that we can neither doubt their information nor their veracity; that they had opportunities sufficient to be assured of the fact, and honesty incapable of forging and propagating falsehood; that they could not be themselves deceived, nor were capable of practising deception upon others; and that their accounts are faithfully transmitted down to us; then, have we all the evidence which a fact so remote can possibly admit.

That the evangelical records or books of the New Testament which contain those accounts, are genuine and authentic, written in the apostolic age, by those persons, the followers and disciples of CHRIST, under whose names we receive them, appears from the testimony of many ancient writers, who were cotemporary, or nearly so, with the authors of those books; not only among Christians, who frequently quote and transcribe parts of them in their works, but among the avowed adversaries

ries of Christianity, Jewish and Heathen writers, who never called their authenticity in question, but expresly admit and mention them as the works of those sacred authors to whom they are ascribed, though they had an aversion to the religious system they taught, and their prejudices and interest urged them to disprove it.

That these sacred writings are, moreover, faithfully transmitted down to us, without any material corruption or adulteration, **appears** from a variety of circumstances; **from** the high estimation and reverence in which they were ever held by Christians, who always regarded them as the sacred rule of their faith and conduct; from their being frequently and publicly read in Christian assemblies, as part of their public devotions; from the early translation of them into most of the known languages of the world, and the agreement and harmony of such translations; **from** the quotations made from them, still remaining in ancient writers; from the constant appeals made to them by various sects

sects of Christians, in matters of controversy; for which reason, there could be no material adulteration inserted, either by the artifice of particular sects, or by common combination and consent. So that there is no room to doubt, but that the books of the New Testament are authentic, written by the persons to whom they are ascribed; and that likewise they have been transmitted down to us, through a long succession of ages, in their genuine and original purity.

We may, in the next place, observe, that the Apostles must have had a clear conviction of the certainty of our blessed Lord's ascension. In this their constant attendance on him made it altogether impossible they should be deceived. For his ascension was not quick and sudden, such as might possibly carry the appearance of illusion; but it was slow and gradual: for when he had spoken, while they beheld, which implies their fixed and steady view of his ascension, while they were pursuing him with eager eyes, he was taken up, and

a cloud

a cloud received him out of their sight. And while they looked stedfastly towards heaven as he went up, behold two men, inhabitants probably of the **heavenly region whither** he had ascended, stood by them in **white** apparel, and said, *Ye men of Galilee, why stand ye gazing towards heaven? This same Jesus which is taken from you, shall so come, in like manner as ye have seen him go into heaven.*

The apostles could not here be deceived **by any artifice or illusion.** For, if seeing the everlasting doors of heaven opened to receive the King of glory; if seeing him ascend, and make the light his garment, and the clouds the chariot of his triumph; if having the evidence of sight confirmed by the voice of angels;—if these are convincing circumstances of a true real ascension, then were the apostles sufficiently assured of what they **so resolutely** asserted.

And as a corroborative proof, that, when he was taken from them, and a cloud received him out of their sight, there was

no

no deception or impofition on the fenfes, they were in a few days convinced by the moft fenfible effects, when they found themfelves vefted, as he had promifed, with miraculous powers, and were enabled to execute his command of teaching all nations, by the gift conferred on them of fpeaking in all languages. They could then no longer doubt, that his prediction was verified; that he was gone to the FATHER, and had all power committed to him both in heaven and earth.

But further: As the apoftles were fufficiently affured of the truth of our SAVIOUR's afcenfion, fo did they tranfmit a faithful account of it to fucceeding ages. For, befides the incredibility of fuppofing a few illiterate perfons capable of planning and conducting an impofition of that nature and confequence, which, they might be fure, would not be implicitly received, they difcover, in their narration, all the internal marks and evidences of veracity, all the characters of artlefs undifguifed probity, and impartial regard for truth,

that

that any writings can possibly be supposed to contain. They record their own errors with a plain and honest integrity: they relate, not only the meanness of their birth, condition, and circumstances; but their ignorance, their prejudices, their ambition, their mutual contentions, and the reproofs they received from their LORD. The undisguised relation of the denial of one apostle, of the treachery of another, of the unbelief of a third, and of the desertion of them all, affords no small presumption, that they had no other interest at heart than that of truth.

But should we suppose them capable of propagating an imposture in the world, which yet the discerning jealousy of the Jews would have rendered impracticable; what prospects could invite, what conceivable motives tempt, them to project or carry on the fraud? Was the doctrine of a suffering, crucified Master, likely to procure ease, or affluence, or honour, to his disciples? *Marvel not if the world hate you*, was their Master's caution; *the servant is not greater than his master, nor the disciple than his Lord.* They saw what severities the Jews had inflicted on the Founder of Christianity. What expectations, then, of favour or success could they form, **by asserting** the visible ascension, and reception into heaven, of him **whom** their countrymen with wicked hands had crucified and slain? This might prove fatal to those who should upbraid a nation with a fact which would fix and perpetuate reproach and infamy upon it, but never could ingratiate or recommend them.

This the apostles well knew; for their Lord had informed them, that the time was coming, that whosoever should kill them would think that he did God service: And yet, notwithstanding they saw not only opposition and persecution, **not** only bonds and imprisonment, but even death, in all its various forms of terror, awaiting the declaration of so unwelcome a truth, they persisted in their testimony **with** an unshaken constancy; and with the most persevering and determined assiduity, continued to publish, that CHRIST was ascended into heaven, far above all principalities and powers. All the Apostles and Evangelists, St John only excepted, sealed their testimony with their blood, and laid down their lives in confirmation of what they attested and taught.

As, then, we have the unanimous testimony of persons, who by the evidence of their own sight, confirmed by the voice of angels, were assured of our SAVIOUR's ascension; as they were persons incapable of forming and conducting any artful design; as it was a doctrine which, if false, could be productive of no advantage to the propagators of it; and as they persevered in asserting it, in despite of all the tortures that cruelty could devise, or power inflict; we have the fullest evidence of the certainty of our SAVIOUR's ascension that the nature of the fact can admit, or in reason we can require.

I shall conclude with some inferences suggested by this doctrine.

1*st*, The ascension of our LORD into Heaven,

Heaven, is to be confidered as an indubitable conclufive evidence of the truth of his doctrine, and of his divine miffion and authority. If we could continue diffident of his pretenfions and character, after all the atteftations given, all the evidences of a miraculous and divine power exhibited in his life and in his death, yet his vifible afcent and reception into glory muft extinguifh all doubts, and place the truth of his doctrine and miffion above all exception. For it is utterly inconfiftent with the character and perfections of the Supreme BEING, to mark with his approbation, in fo confpicuous and miraculous a manner, one who, unauthorifed, had affumed a divine commiffion, and, under an ufurped authority, had delivered doctrines and precepts which were not agreeable to his will.

2*dly,* If CHRIST is afcended into heaven, then we have a perpetual Patron and Advocate there, to plead our caufe, to intercede in our favour, and to render our Supreme JUDGE propitious to all that are truly

truly penitent. We may be assured, that he will not fail to ask those blessings which he purchased with the effusion of his blood. What may we not hope for from the intercession of so compassionate and powerful a Mediator, if we endeavour to purify our minds from all iniquity, and render ourselves worthy of his intercession?

Lastly, The doctrine of our SAVIOUR's ascension may administer abundant matter of consolation and holy joy to us his followers, who ought to consider his ascension as the earnest and pledge of our own. For thus he assures his disciples, *I go to prepare a place for you; and will come again, and receive you up to myself; that where I am, there ye may be also.* This promise he will undoubtedly fulfil to all the disciples of his righteousness; and, at his last coming down from heaven, in the same manner as he went up to heaven, will change our vile bodies, that they may be like unto his glorious body, and will

will set us at his own right hand in heavenly places.

We have the best grounds for dependence on his promise, since his other predictions were verified and completed. He foretold his own resurrection and ascension, and foretold ours; the one to happen in a short time, and the other not till the final consummation of all things. He himself rose from the dead, and ascended into heaven, according to his own prediction: and we cannot need a more certain and undoubted pledge, that our corruptible bodies shall likewise in due time put on incorruption; that he will receive us to himself; and that where he is, there we shall be also.

Let this hope, then, encourage and animate us to look up to heaven, and to have our conversation there. Let us not suffer our minds to be chained down to the concernments of this life; but let us elevate them often to higher objects, to things celestial and eternal. Let us often, on the wings of holy contemplation, follow our

Lord and Saviour; and in heart and mind afcend whither he is gone before us, and where our fouls, when unfettered from this world, will, we hope, dwell with him, amidft fullnefs of joy, to eternal ages.

SERMON XIII.

On Divine GRACE, and Human Co-operation.

PHIL. ii. 12, 13.

*Work out your own salvation with fear and trembling: **for it is God that worketh in you, both to will and to do of his good pleasure.***

OPINIONS have been divided in the Chriſtian church, concerning the extent, influence, and efficacy, of Divine Grace, and the power and liberty of the Human Will. Some have aſſerted, that, in the preſent degenerate ſtate of human nature, it is not poſſible for us, by our own

own exertions, to act any effectual part in the work of our falvation: that divine grace does all, and we can do nothing for ourfelves: that the Spirit of GOD moves the fprings of action in us by a fecret, unfelt, but a powerful and irrefiftible hand: that he acts upon the mind, not indeed like an impetuous torrent, violently and vifibly bearing down our liberty of will; but as a fmooth and gentle ftream, which, with an effectual, though imperceptible force, carries us along with it: that all our virtues and good actions derive, confequently, their whole merit from his agency, and are the produce of his operations.

But, according to this opinion, we are mere machines or inftruments in the hands of a fuperior agent; our beft performances, confequently, can have no moral value, nor be entitled to approbation or reward. For what reward, what approbation, can we claim for actions which are not ours, but wrought and produced in us by a fuperior direction?

On the contrary, others, by afferting the

the unreftricted, uninfluenced freedom of the will, and our entire and abfolute ability of choofing good or evil, have been thought to derogate from the power and efficacy of a divine grace. For certain it is, that nature, unaided by grace, is not of itfelf fufficient to holinefs. The corruption of our nature is a bias that inclines us to vice: a principle above nature is requifite to counteract this propenfion, and draw us to virtue.

The Scripture accordingly informs us, that we are not fufficient of ourfelves, but that our fufficiency is of God; that without him, we can do nothing; that it is he that worketh in us both to will and to do. This corruption and depravation of human nature is not a difcovery that we owe to Revelation; it was always the general fenfe of mankind; the beft and wifeft of the Heathens have obferved, acknowledged, and lamented it; we all but too much feel it in ourfelves, and may obferve it in others.

But notwithftanding it is admitted that

that our sufficiency is of God, and that it is he that worketh in us both to will and to do; yet we are not to be merely passive under the divine influences: some part must belong to ourselves in the work of our salvation. Why else are we exhorted not to receive the grace of God in vain? why forbidden to quench or grieve the Holy Spirit! why commanded to work out our salvation with fear and trembling? and to what end are all the precepts and exhortations of the Scriptures? There is therefore, doubtless, required a joint efficiency and co-operation of the divine assistance, and our own agency, to the accomplishment of our salvation.

This idea is expressed in the words of the text; where the apostle does not say, Work out your salvation yourselves, for you have no need of divine grace; nor does he say, on the other hand, The divine grace does all, and therefore you need do nothing yourselves: but, ascribing to each its proper office, he says,
Work

Work out your own falvation, becaufe divine grace gives you power fo to do.

I fhall in this difcourfe confider the extent of divine grace and human liberty, and point out the diftinct province of each; and fhow in what refpects our good actions are to be attributed to the Supreme BEING, and how far they are to be afcribed to ourfelves.

In the following refpects, then, our actions may be afcribed to GOD.——Firft, From GOD, the original Author of every good gift, we derive all our powers; and on his fuftaining hand we depend for the prefervation and exercife of them. All our intentions, determinations, and actions, though under the immediate direction of our will, yet are exerted under HIM, without whofe concurrence we can neither act, nor think, nor move, nor have our being. As GOD, then, originally imparted, and ftill continues to fupport, our powers of acting, our actions may in one fenfe, or ultimately, be afcribed to him.

But befides thofe powers granted us by Nature,

Nature, together with our being, GOD is pleased to illuminate our minds by the immediate aids and influences of his Holy Spirit. The nature of these influences, and their mode of operation on the understanding, we cannot ascertain with precision: but they should seem to consist, in invigorating our intellectual powers; or in arranging our ideas in such order, and placing them in such a light, that we may have a clearer discernment of religious doctrines or duties than we should otherwise acquire; or in recalling to our consideration important and forgotten truths, and giving them a deeper impression on the mind.

But further: The DEITY not only aids our understandings, but influences also our wills and affections, by presenting to them the most powerful motives, by operating on our hopes and fears, setting before us future inflictions and rewards, suggesting pious sentiments, prompting us to virtuous resolutions, communicating inward assistance and ability to all the purposes

poses of holiness and obedience, and disposing our hearts to the reception of divine truths. As GOD, in the former case, illuminates our understandings, by opening, as it were, the eye of the soul, and giving us a clear prospect and discernment of our duty and its obligations; so here he influences and bends our inclinations to the observance of duty, by powerful motives: motives that operate on the mind, not indeed with a compulsive force, but with all the force that can be offered to the liberty of moral agents; all the force that is consistent with the nature of duty; all the force that can attend admonition, exhortation, conviction.

The opinion and belief of a supernatural assistance is so reasonable, so consonant to our ideas of the divine goodness and of human frailty, that philosophers, even in the Heathen world, were sensible how much it was wanted, and have expressly asserted, that, without divine assistance, no man could make a progress either in wisdom or virtue. What Reason suggested to
them,

them, Revelation has ascertained to us; which represents us as temples and habitations of the Holy Spirit.

It may appear, then, what share may properly be ascribed to God in the production of our good works; and it is easy to discover what remains on our part, and is required from us to do for ourselves. The Supreme Being does not overrule our liberty; nor, like a despotic sovereign, chain down our will to his determinations; but, as a friend, addresses us, and prevails by the gentle force of rational and moral influence. He first gives us sufficient powers and abilities to act; and then invites us to a right exertion of those powers, by offering the most effectual inducements, by presenting to our view the reasonableness, the amiableness, the obligations, the happiness, of religious obedience. He enables, admonishes, and exhorts us to discharge our various duties; we ought to attend to his admonitions, and comply with his influences. He furnishes the means of action, and motives for acting;

acting: in consequence of these, it is our province to deliberate, to determine, and to act.

God does not irresistibly turn the balance of our will, nor absolutely determine our actions: for then they would be his actions, not ours; he would be the sole agent, we only the instruments he employs. Whatever may be the nature of the divine influences, or their manner of operation on the mind; however our understandings may be illuminated or our affections rectified;—we may be assured, that we retain our moral liberty; that our intentions and actions are left, generally, to our own determination; that we have the government of ourselves; and that our whole behaviour is at our own disposal; which circumstance alone it is that can render us accountable for it.

Our SAVIOUR, in order to describe the influence and operation of divine grace upon his followers, represents it under the similitude of a vine and its branches. *I am the vine,* says he, *ye are the branches:*

he that abideth in me, and I in him, the same bringeth forth much fruit. As there is a natural, vital union, between the vine and the branches, so is there a spiritual union between CHRIST and his true disciples, on which the communication of his grace and spirit depends. The mystical Vine conveys to every branch a vital principle, a constant supply of spiritual nutriment; it belongs to us the branches, in virtue of these communications from the root, to contribute our part to the production of fruit.

The same idea is illustrated in the parable of the Sower; where the seed sown is the word of GOD, the rain from heaven denotes the divine assistance; yet still the produce is represented to be in proportion to the natural fertility and goodness of the soil. The ALMIGHTY confers his assistance, and bears a part in our salvation; but we are not thence to infer, that his assistance will do all, without our own efforts.

Our nature is indeed weak and frail,
too

too easily seduced by the temptations we can resist; too prone to evil, though we can discern and choose the good; too inattentive to the divine suggestions, but not incapable of complying and co-operating with them. Let us not dishonour our MAKER, by supposing that he has made us totally corrupt, that he has formed and fitted us only for sin, and left every ingredient of good out of the human composition. Let us not suppose, that we can add to his glory by degrading his works; by degrading man, the chief of his works within our sphere of observation. It is GOD, indeed, that worketh in us both to will and to do; yet we are required, and consequently have power, to work out our salvation. Our labours cannot avail without his assistance; his assistance will not avail without our labours; on the concurrence of both, our virtue now, and our felicity hereafter, depend.

It may appear, then, in what sense the scripture is to be understood, when it attributes our good works both to GOD and to ourselves. He illuminates our understanding; and by a secret influence, suggests, and excites us to, what is right: in consequence of this ability and assistance, we determine and act. He instructs us, and invites our obedience, by the natural light of our own minds, by the express revelation of his will, and by the secret whispers and suggestions of his Holy Spirit. But the success of all these methods will turn upon our complying with, or rejecting, them. We may attend, or not, to the admonitions of our own mind; we may observe, or neglect, his revealed instructions; we may yield to, or oppose, the impulses of the Holy Spirit.

God does not with a resistless hand compel us into his service. All his assistances require our own concurrence, to render them effectual. His grace will not illuminate our minds, if we industriously bar them against light and truth. If we have ears to hear, and will not hear, the divine instructions are given in vain.

But we ought to consider, that when
God

God invites and offers to conduct us to duty and happiness, if we are unwilling to comply, if we refuse his invitation and reject his assistance, our case is then indeed desperate, and without remedy: for as it is inconsistent with the nature of virtue to suppose that we can be made virtuous and good by compulsion; so it is inconsistent with the nature and perfections of God to suppose, that without virtue or goodness he will approve or reward us.

If we repay his favour with ingratitude, and continue unprofitable under the means of grace, God, instead of compelling us, by an over-ruling direction into the paths of obedience and happiness, may be provoked to resume his slighted gifts, and withhold the grace which we receive in vain. And nothing more is requisite to our certain undoing, than to be forsaken of him, and his assisting grace to be withdrawn. Were it our unhappy lot to be thus exposed, defenceless, to the assaults of temptation; left to encounter the adversaries of our happiness, destitute of divine armour;

armour; cut off from all communication with God; all supplies of his grace intercepted; the frailty and corruption of our nature would soon betray and give us up into the enemy's hands. Unsupported by divine assistance, we should be lost to every good disposition, lost to every virtue. Like branches lopped off and severed from the vine, we should lose the vital principle that renders us productive of moral fruit; we should be cast forth, and withered, and fitted for destruction.

On the other hand, if we bend our minds to a compliance with the will of our heavenly FATHER, and are obedient to his direction and guidance, his powerful, though unseen arm, will conduct us from virtue to virtue; and will never be wanting to us, if we are not wanting to ourselves. If we open our hearts to his sacred influences; if our souls gasp unto him as a thirsty land, and drink in the dew of his spirit as it silently descends upon us from heaven; we shall then be neither barren nor unfruitful: the seed
of

of divine grace thus sown upon good ground, upon its natural and proper soil, an honest and good heart, will take root and be productive of the genuine fruits of the Spirit,—the graces and virtues of a good life.

Grace is the greatest, best, of Heaven's blessings; and far transcends all others we can enjoy. Temporal good things God promiscuously bestows on the just and the unjust; often on the evil and unthankful, on those who neither solicit nor acknowledge his favours. But his grace he accounts a pearl of greater price than to be thrown to the negligent and undeserving. He gives it only to them that ask it; to them who piously implore, and justly prize the heavenly gift. Would we then obtain of God a blessing as requisite to our growth in goodness, to the sustenance of our spiritual life, as is our daily bread to that of the body; let us not neglect to approach him with importunate and fervent supplications for it.

For the attainment of this blessing, this

spiritual food, our prayers cannot be too fervent, cannot be too importunate. And happy, sure, is the lot of Christians, to whom God has promised the assistance of his Holy Spirit, on the easy terms of asking, and gratefully receiving it; happy that we are not left altogether to the power of irregular passions, to the protection of our own weakness, and to the counsels of our own corruption; happy that we are under the eye and superintendance of so powerful, yet so kind, a guardian,—who never forsakes, till he is forsaken by us; never withdraws his assistance, till we render it ineffectual; never abandons us in temptations, till our own hearts take part with the tempter, and we betray ourselves; never refuses his grace, till we receive it in vain!

Let us not, then, be wanting to ourselves in supplicating and complying with the influences of this divine instructor; and *forasmuch as without thee, O God, we are not able to please thee, mercifully grant,*

grant, that thy Holy Spirit **may in** all things direct and rule our hearts, **that in** keeping thy commandments we may please thee, both in will and deed, through Jesus Christ our Lord.

SERMON XIV.

Againſt an improper Love of this World.

1 JOHN ii. 15.

Love not the world, neither the things that are in the world.

NO enemy exiſts more fatal to virtue and religion, and conſequently to to our higheſt and beſt intereſt, than an intemperate paſſion for the world and its enjoyments. That is the fountain from whence iſſue all the vices and iniquities of mankind. But the deſign of Religion is, to
inform

inform us of the worth and dignity of the foul, and of the nature of our chief good and happinefs; to moderate our attachment to the world; and, by calling off our thoughts from its falfe and fading pleafures, to direct and elevate them to where true and permanent joys are to be found. An undue love of the world counteracts and defeats thefe purpofes; renders us inattentive to, and unworthy of, our proper happinefs; and at the fame time corrupts and vitiates the mind, and difqualifies and unfits it even for relifhing and tafting it.

Neceffary, therefore, it is, that we fhould be often cautioned againft an intemperate love of the world; a vice fo powerful in its temptations, and fo fatal in its effects. And indeed, if, in the very days of our Lord and his apoftles, when, with regard to the evidence of a future ftate, men may be almoft faid to have walked by fight and not by faith, and, by the doctrines which they heard, and the miracles they faw, to have had heaven and the glories of another world almoft laid open to view—

if

if under these advantageous circumstances it was necessary to be cautioned against the allurements and delusions of the world, much more proper is the admonition, more needful the caution, now. But here let it be observed, that the love of the world is not in every sense culpable. We are not to understand the apostle, by the words in the text, as forbidding that regard and value for temporal things, which the present state and condition of life render necessary. For though earthly things cannot constitute felicity, are not the materials of true happiness; yet they are the kind provisions and prescriptions which our gracious CREATOR has given us against bodily wants and miseries, and are to be received and acknowledged with grateful sentiments of his goodness. To consult our well-being here, is a dictate of the law of nature, as well as to provide for our happiness hereafter. They who, from the apostle's prohibition of loving the world, would infer, that we should hate it, make a very unnatural and wrong conclusion. For

were

were any thing criminal in diligence and industry in acquiring, or in moderation and temperance in enjoying, the good things of the world, our nature would then be finful; it would be criminal to be a human being; and we might have juft reafon to fay to our MAKER, *Why haft thou made me thus?*

In order, therefore, to have a right conception of the meaning and extent of the prohibition in the text, *Love not the world;* we muft confider what could be the defign of our MAKER in the formation of the world, and for what end and purpofe he placed us in it: for hence only can we determine of what real worth and value the world is to us, as this depends folely upon the will and pleafure of our CREATOR.

GOD's principal defign in our creation fhould feem to be, to form us to a capacity of enjoying himfelf; of being with him, in a manner at prefent above our conception; and, perhaps, to fupply and fill up the ftations of other beings, from which they

they by transgression have fallen. In order to this advancement and promotion, the necessary requisites and qualifications are, such a rectitude of mind and will, such a conformity and likeness to the Supreme BEING, and such dispositions of virtue and holiness, as are no other way attainable, but in a state of discipline and probation.

For this end and purpose our CREATOR seems to have assigned the station and condition in which we now find ourselves; to have clothed us with a body, with inclinations and passions; and to have placed us in this world, in order to prepare, and form, and train us up, for heaven and himself. And that the law in our members might yield sufficient scope and occasion for the law of the mind to exercise and exert itself, GOD has made this world every way fit for a probationary state; fit to answer his purpose, both in providing a supply for lawful and regular desires, and temptation to such as are unlawful and irregular; that we might by this means

prove

prove and exert our fidelity and obedience to him. And in this fenfe, the tree of the knowledge of good and evil is growing ftill, and we are ftill tempted with forbidden fruit.

This being confidered, it is eafy to apprehend when the love of the world becomes criminal. And this it certainly does, when we confider it as our fole or principal good; when it has influence enough to feduce us to thofe vices that difqualify us for the prefence and enjoyment of the Beft and moft Perfect of Beings; when we have recourfe to any arts of fraud or violence to obtain its honours, riches, or pleafures; when we poffefs this world's goods, and yet fee and fuffer our fellow-creatures to labour under the want of what we penurioufly accumulate, or profufely fquander; or when we are averfe to bid adieu to the world at the command of our MAKER; when we yield with reluctance to the laft fummons that calls us hence, and are unwilling to refign our foul to him that gave it. When the love of the world

world betrays us into any of these impieties, we not only love it better than we ought to do, but indeed better than we do ourselves; and the world with all its glories, could we possess them, would make us but poor amends for what we shall lose by this imprudent attachment to it.

For to have GOD always before our eyes, as our sole and principal good; to be kind and compassionate to our fellow-creatures; and, with pious resignation, to say to HIM who best knows what is good for us, *Thy will be done;*—these are all great and indispensable points of duty, virtues which in this life we are to exercise and practise; and are some of those prerequisites and preparatory qualifications for happiness, which we are sent here on purpose to acquire, and without which we cannot hope to see the face of GOD in glory. So that this world, far from being the first and principal object of our affections, should ever be beheld with a jealous and a cautious eye.

There is danger in indulging even a legitimate

gitimate love of the world; it is apt to infinuate and become the favourite paſſion, to withdraw our affection from God, and tempt us to defert his fervice. The Scripture reprefents the world as a region where every path is befet with fnares fatal to our future expectations; where we muſt walk with fear and circumfpection, with the conſtant vigilance and apprehenſions of thofe who travel through an enemy's country. We are often reminded of its feducements and dangers; and that life is one continued conflict with temptations.

But it may here be afked, Is not the fuppofition of this world's being defigned as a tempter to evil, a prompter to immoral and diſhoneſt defires, is not this an impeachment of the holinefs and goodnefs of the Creator? Do we not hereby, in the final iffue, make God a tempter to evil, contrary to all our natural apprehenfions of the purity of his moral nature, and to the moſt exprefs declarations of Scripture, which forbid us, when we are tempted, to fay that we are tempted of God?

To

To which it may be replied, That if the trying and bringing our virtue to the test may be called tempting us to evil, GOD may in this sense be justly said to tempt his creatures; for both Reason and Scripture agree, that the present life is intended as a state of trial and probation, preparatory to another. But the trial and proof of our virtue is very improperly called a temptation to evil; because, upon the whole, much more powerful are the incitement to virtue than to vice. So that GOD cannot justly be said to tempt us to evil, but to good; inasmuch as Heaven, with which GOD has promised to reward virtue and goodness, is a much more powerful allurement, or temptation, if it may have that name, than any other consideration can possibly be.

For what reasons our CREATOR has thought fit to set before us any temptations to evil; why he placed creatures, so fallible and so frail as we, in a situation exposed to any the least hazard or danger; is indeed a difficulty in speculation. But the

the state of the case should seem to be this. Our MAKER's principal design in the creation of man (as was before observed), seems to be that of forming a creature to be with himself, and to participate in his happiness. But before man can be admitted to the vision and enjoyment of GOD, it is necessary that he be holy; and to be holy, he must first pass through a state of trial. This makes some such state as we are now in, in this world, to become necessary; where the motives and inducements to virtue and vice are so wisely balanced, and so duly proportioned, that our preference of either may be a matter of mere choice, and the determination of a most free agent.

And this state of probation, this setting of evil as well as good before us, and putting happiness or misery equally in our power, is not a hardship peculiar to human nature: it is probable, that it either now is, or has been, the case of every created, intelligent being; that none have been placed in the full possession of happiness at first, but have been trained to it by a trial of their obedience; and that there is no creature now in heaven, where the good and virtuous shall one day be, but has passed through some such introductory state of discipline and probation as the good and virtuous now do in this world. For moral goodness is essential to the happiness of a moral being; and there seems to be a like necessary relation between a state of probation and moral goodness. Take away all trial and temptation to vice, where will be the merit of virtue, or to what reward can it be entitled? Temptations to vice, by furnishing opportunities for the trial and exercise of virtue, add both to our present merit and to our future happiness; and the more powerful those temptations are, and the stronger our resolution to oppose them, the greater is our virtue, and the more glorious will be our reward.

Let us then often and seriously consider what we are, to what end created, for what purpose the AUTHOR of our being
has

has set good and evil, life and death, before us; and placed us here, as in a pleasant garden indeed, but planted with forbidden fruit; not surely that we should eat and die, but rather that we should refrain and live: not that we should let go our integrity, and sell our heavenly inheritance, our birthright, for a morsel of power, wealth, or pleasure; but that it should appear by our behaviour, by a vigilant, uniform, and determined obedience to our MAKER, that our regard to him is infinitely superior to all worldly considerations, and that there is nothing upon earth that we desire in comparison of him.

The motives of religion says an excellent author *, ought at all times to have so much influence as to prevail over the temptations to sin; and it is not our infirmity but our iniquity, if they do it not. Our passions and appetites, our employment and our company, our youth or our age, the examples of those we con-

* Dr Clarke.

verse with, or the fashionable and customary vices of our country;—these, and the like, are the temptations which it is the business of religion, and the proper trial of our virtue, to overcome. And if our passions betray, or company seduce, or the customs and fashion of the world lead us carelesly and inconsiderately into the ways of destruction, it is not our excuse, but our condemnation, that we have followed a multitude to do evil; that we have been prevailed upon more by the influence of the world, than by the fear of God; or that our affection to sin has been so strong, that reason and religion have not been able to subdue it.

Let God, then, be the supreme object of our affection; let nothing be regarded, in comparison to the duty we owe to him, nor suffered to come in competition with it. Let us wisely reject what would be most agreeable, pleasant, and beneficial, whenever the acquisition, if we have it not, or the possession, if we have it, is inconsistent with duty, and with the regard we owe to the ALMIGHTY; that thus we may fecure our future happinefs, and fo pafs through things temporal, as finally to lofe not the things eternal.

May that all-powerful BEING, who alone can order the wills and affections of finful men, grant, that we may love what he commands, and defire what he does promife, that fo, among the fundry and manifold changes of the world, our hearts may furely there be fixed where true joys are to be found!

SERMON XV.

Sin of profaning the Name of GOD.

LEVIT. xix. 12.

Ye shall not swear by my name falsely, neither shalt thou profane the name of thy God.

RELIGION, among other advantages it brought to society, has consulted its security and welfare, by furnishing the firmest bond of fidelity, and laying men under the strictest obligation to reverence an oath, on which the public peace and safety so much depend, that neither character, nor property, nor life, can be secure, where the obligation of an oath is
not

not held sacred, and the violation of it dreaded. But such is the corruption of mankind, that this basis of truth and justice is too often made to support iniquity and falsehood, and this sacred tie too often sported with.

From the words of the text I shall take occasion to show, 1*st*, What is the nature of an oath; 2*dly*, What it is to profane the name of God; and *lastly*, Shall offer some considerations on the guilt of habitually profaning his sacred name in conversation.

I. An oath is an appeal to the Supreme Being, as judge of the truth of what we assert; whose omniscience knows the secrets of our hearts, knows whether what we declare be correspondent or not to the conviction of our minds; and whose justice will accordingly either favour, or be avenged of us: it is the submitting to God, the invisible Judge; and imploring his protection, or imprecating his vengeance, according to the truth or falsehood of what we affirm. Such is the solemn nature of an oath; and therefore we should always consider well what we are engaged in, whenever we invoke the Supreme Judge of the world as a witness to our assertions.

II. Let us, in the next place, observe what it is to profane the name of GOD. This is done when we use it without due consideration and reverence, or when we use it in an unlawful action. The sacred name of GOD carries in it the idea of such infinite and inconceivable perfection, of such supreme majesty, power and authority, that it ought never to be pronounced but with respectful veneration. It should not find admission into our conversation, but when our minds are engaged in pious sentiments, and our expressions are serious and devout.

We are directed to sanctify the LORD our GOD, *i. e.* to form such holy conceptions of his great and adorable nature, as may lead us to a suitable return of reverential homage. And yet how common is it, on the moſt flight and unimportant occaſions, to hear men utter inconſiderately the name of GOD, when neither the ſubject of their thoughts is ſo weighty, nor the temper of their minds ſo ſerious, as to juſtify the uſe of it! Should we, by a ſeaſonable and well-timed mention of the ſacred name, impreſs on our minds juſt ideas of his ineffable perfections, of the excellencies of his nature, the wonders of his wiſdom, or the mercies of his providence, and thereby affect our hearts with juſt ſentiments of reſpect and veneration, this were to ſanctify his name. But when we idly apply it to light and trivial ſubjects, we then profane it, we proſtitute it to mean and low purpoſes, unſuitable to the greatneſs, unbecoming the dignity, of the divine nature. It muſt ſurely be offenſive to the Supreme SOVEREIGN of the world, who has himſelf informed us that he is a jealous GOD, jealous of his honour, and that he will not ſuffer it to be withheld from him, to obſerve his creatures with a careleſs indifference profane his name,

and

and utter it with all the marks of irreverence and difrefpect.

But further: The name of GOD is in a peculiar manner profaned, when we invoke his prefence to an unlawful action, and fummon him, as it were, to be a fpectator of our guilt. This is a fin of a more than common magnitude; it is an open defiance to the power and juftice of the ALMIGHTY, and an infult on almoft all the perfections of the divine nature. This is a degree of guilt which GOD will certainly punifh with a more than common vengeance. For if he who utters the name of GOD without due reverence, fhall not be found guiltlefs; he who bids defiance to the all-feeing eye and all-powerful arm of the ALMIGHTY, by invoking him as a witnefs to his crimes, may doubtlefs expect ftill feverer inflictions of his juftice.

III. I proceed to offer fome confiderations on the guilt of habitually profaning the name of GOD in converfation. No one inftructed in the firft rudiments of religion can be ignorant of the flagitious nature of

this

this sin. With what a solemn denunciation of divine wrath is the following precept delivered? *Thou shalt not take the name of the Lord thy God in vain; for the Lord will not hold him guiltless that taketh his name in vain.* The precept is full, plain, and express; the judgment denounced against it, severe and terrible. In the New Testament, our SAVIOUR says, *Swear not at all.* And by the vehemence expressed by St James, we may reasonably judge, that he considered this sin of habitually profaning the name of GOD, as a sin of no small weight. *Above all things, my brethren,* says he, *swear not.* But why *above all things*, if not because it is a sin in a peculiar manner hateful and offensive in the sight of GOD? It is a wilful determined transgression, incapable of any extenuation from ignorance or infirmity. We cannot pretend ignorance of a precept known and understood by all. Nor can we plead the infirmity of our nature; for nature has no propensity to this sin. It is a voluntary habit taken up at pleasure, and might in a great meafure be laid down with the fame eafe. This renders it the more culpable, fince it can claim no alleviation either from ignorance or infirmity.

It is recorded as an aggravating circumftance of the leper's contempt of the prophet Elijah's advice, that he refufed to purfue it, though directed to fo eafy a prefcription as to wafh and be clean: *Had the prophet bid thee do fome great thing, wouldft thou not have done it? how much rather, when he only bids thee wafh and be clean?* This is mentioned to fhow the more than common criminality of any finful practice which may with little or no trouble be avoided. Such is the fin of profaning the name of GOD; for here there is no natural inclination to contend againft, no conflict between reafon and paffion. The paffionate man may plead the fire of a warm difpofition; the gloomy fullennefs of the morofe may urge the power of an unhappy complexion; but the profaner of the name of GOD has no fuch plea. Common reafon teaches us to reverence the

majefty

majesty of the Supreme BEING; and no corruption of our nature tempts us to profane that name, which we all know it is our duty to adore.

But further: Besides the guilt of this practice in itself, it unhappily leads to a sin of a still more enormous magnitude;— to that of Perjury. An habitual custom of profaning the name of GOD, abates the respect and reverence men ought to have for an oath. It is not possible they should become proficients in this sin, did they not, by a gradual progress in it, render it easy and familiar; and consequently that awe and reverence which they might once have had for the sacred name, is, by long repeated custom, gradually and insensibly diminished and lost; and then it is but natural to suppose, they grow more indifferent and inattentive to the truth or falsehood of their oath.

This must inevitably happen to those who have so habituated themselves to this sin, that they are often guilty, even without attending to it. And when this practice

tice is become so habitual and familiar, that they can hardly finish a sentence without binding it with an oath; if they thus happen to assert what is false, or promise what they mean not to perform, they involve themselves in the guilt of perjury. And though doubtless many, who by the practice of mingling oaths with their common discourse have been rashly and inadvertently surprised into the guilt of perjury, would detest the commission of that crime upon more deliberate and solemn occasions; yet the frequent instances of that crime, upon such solemn occasions, seem to originate from the habitual practice of profaning the name of GOD in conversation. For few persons are capable of advancing at once to a crime so enormous. But habit and custom gradually wear out the impressions of conscience; and what the mind would at first startle at, practice and long usage may render familiar, and at length possibly agreeable.

This should incline all to contribute their endeavours, by advice, by example,

by

by reproof, or any other method, to suppress the common practice of profaning the name of God; since the pernicious sin of perjury, by which the character, property, or life of any person whatever may be endangered,—a sin which has a tendency to destroy all mutual confidence, and to subvert all civil society,—is in a great degree owing to it.

I shall conclude with some short admonitions, in order to prevent the growth or continuance of this sin.

1*st*, He who would avoid the habit or custom, must beware of the first step or tendency to it. It is a maxim in spiritual as well as bodily disorders, to check the first appearance of a disease, lest it should grow inveterate, and at length incurable. And therefore we should do well to avoid all vehemence of assertion, all violence of passion, as dangerous approaches to this sin. St Peter, charged with being one of the disciples of Jesus, at first replied with a bare denial; accused a second time, he grew somewhat warmer, and expressed
himself

himself with greater vehemence; but when charged the third time, urged his denial with oaths and imprecations.

2dly, We may hence observe the danger of yielding to the first impulses of passion, since even an Apostle, in a short space of time, was led on from a bare denial to bitter and violent imprecations. When the mind is hurried on by the impetuosity of violent passion, oaths are often found the readiest way to discharge the heat of resentment; and the mind, not under the conduct of reason, vents a sinful passion by a more sinful execration.

Lastly, Let us possess our minds with the most respectful and awful sentiments of the greatness and goodness, and majesty of the Supreme BEING. This is the most rational and effectual means to prevent us from prostituting and profaning his sacred name. Is he the LORD and RULER of the universe, who has heaven for his throne, and earth for his footstool, whose power is irresistible, whose kingdom is infinite and eternal, whose sovereignty

reignty gives him a right to our obedience, and whose goodness and mercy to us demand an infinitely higher tribute of grateful respect than we can pay? Let us not dare to offer such an insult and indignity, as to call him to witness every unimportant matter we may happen to be engaged in. Let us ever preserve an awful and reverential regard for the majesty of Heaven; let us not speak or think of GOD but with veneration; let the words of our mouth, as well as the meditations of our heart, be ever acceptable in his sight; let us ever consult his honour, and *hallowed be his name.*

SERMON XVI.

Duty of doing to others, as we would they should do unto us.

MATTH. vii. 12.

All things whatsoever ye would that men should do unto you, do ye even so to them; for this is the law and the prophets.

THE whole system of Christian duties is clearly a reasonable service; perfectly consonant to the natural sentiments of our minds; well adapted to the constitution of human nature, and to the true interest and happiness of mankind; and is marked with evident signatures of the wisdom and benignity of its Author. A-
mong

mong many other excellent laws and precepts contained in it, this in the text, from the high character which our Lord has given it,—from its extenfive utility, and from the foundation it has in equity and reafon,—feems in a peculiar manner to claim attention: *All things whatfoever ye would that men fhould do unto you, do ye even fo to them; for this is the law and the prophets.*

In confidering which words, I fhall obferve, 1*ft*, The true import and extent of this precept; 2*dly*, The reafonablenefs and equity of it; and, *laftly*, Its utility and excellence.

I. I am to confider the true import and extent of this precept; which, excellent as it is, is yet capable of being perverted to purpofes very different from the defign and intention of it. A magiftrate, *e. g.* is not by this precept obliged, or authorifed, to fuffer the guilty to meet with that lenity or impunity, which, in the fame criminal fituation he might probably enough defire to be extended to himfelf. A perfon in power or authority is not bound by this rule to gratify unreasonable expectations in his dependents; though, if himself were in their circumstances, his own desires might perhaps be unreasonable, equally as theirs. It was not the intention of the precept, to constitute our inclinations and desires the rule of our actions, or the standard of right and wrong; but to instruct us, To treat each other, in all circumstances, according to reason and equity; and to observe, in all cases, that behaviour to others, which, on similar occasions, we could with justice and reason expect to receive from them.

It does not lay down any new injunction, or prescribe any duty to which we were not under an antecedent obligation: but it is meant to regulate the practice of all the known social duties; to prescribe the proportion, and ascertain the measure, of justice, mercy, or benevolence, which we ought to mete out to others upon all occasions; and to make that principle of self-love, which is the general occasion of
in-

injustice, fraud, oppression, and iniquity, the most effectual means of pointing out and prompting us to acts of honesty, humanity, and justice. For though it is easy, from our natural sentiments of justice and equity, to discern how far actions are right or wrong, when their consequences are indifferent to us; yet, where ideas of interest interfere, where there is the remotest consideration of self, connected with the point before us, it is no easy task to disengage the mind from that connection. Our passions and inclinations are called in as counsellors, and they have an imperceptible influence even upon the best minds; they are ever ready to offer some flattering insinuation, some favourable circumstance, some colourable pretext, to justify and approve in ourselves what we would disapprove and censure in another.

A slight attention to what passes in the world, may discover many instances of self-partiality, particularly where interest is concerned. Under this influence, we see men biassed in their judgment, and misled; we see them proof against conviction; we see them guilty of flagrant injustice, evident to others, though not seen through that delusive mist which self-love spreads over the understanding. In order, therefore, to guard against this seductive influence, and to enable us to see our conduct in a just light, we should do well to consider ourselves, not as actors, but spectators of our own conduct: we should change the point of view, place our actions at a proper distance, and represent them as done by others; and from this new station we may form a more impartial and equitable judgment of them.

It is to check that partiality, then, so apt always to give its determination in our own favour, that we are directed in the text to make it the rule of our behaviour, To do to others as we should think it reasonable they should do to us. This precept puts us into a capacity of judging impartially between ourselves and others, and, as far as may be, of feeling for them as for ourselves. It makes us in imagination change conditions with them; and places us in a situation where we may have the same equal discernment of their rights and claims as of our own.———Which leads me,

II. To consider the equity and reasonableness of this precept.—To do to others what we would they should do to us, is so clearly just and reasonable, that it requires no elaborate proof or illustration. The mind assents, as soon as it is proposed; it carries its own evidence along with it; every one's conscience naturally acquiesces in it; and all sects, parties, and distinctions of men, are unanimous in subscribing to the equity of it.—The reasonableness of this rule, in all cases of social intercourse, is apparent. Do we wish that others should treat us with benevolence and candour; that they should offer no unprovoked injuries or insults, nor refuse the good offices that friendship or humanity call for? All this every man thinks perfectly reasonable in his own case, and is equally so in the case of all.

Should interest, humour, or passion, then, at any time, as too often they do, prompt us to an injurious or unkind action; ought we not to suspend our compliance till we have consulted and asked our heart, whether we should think it reasonable to suffer that injustice or unkindness ourselves, which we are meditating against another? And every picture of behaviour which in this light appears full of horror and deformity, should be an occasion of dissuading us from those actions which would bring the same disagreeable representation to the mind of our neighbour.

Do we desire that others, in all transactions with us, should adhere to honesty, integrity, and truth? If they insnare us, by fraudulent declarations, ambiguous expressions, or fallacious promises; do we not think it just to exclaim against such injurious treatment? and do we not suppose, that our complaints will be thought
well-

well-grounded, and that the public voice will concur with our own in condemning it? How unreasonable, then, would it be, to have recourse to the same insidious methods which we condemn in others, or to exercise those arts of fraud which we so much resent, when practised upon ourselves? If, again, we have been surprised into some misbehaviour, by passion, mistake, or inadvertence, do we not think a kind construction of it reasonable? and do we not wish to be forgiven? We cannot, then, think it equitable to refuse the same favourable construction, and the same forgiveness, to others, in similar circumstances.

In order, therefore, to act agreeably to reason, and to the social state of our nature, as well as to the injunctions of the Gospel, we should make our SAVIOUR's rule the subject of frequent meditation; *Whatsoever ye would that men should do unto you, do ye even so unto them.* This is an explanation of that other precept, of loving our neighbour as ourselves; which is no-

thing

thing else but a variation of the expreſſion in the text, being the ſame thing in practice. For this reaſon, it is ſaid to be the law and the prophets: not that this rule is ever mentioned in either; nor is it meant, that it comprehends the whole ſyſtem of religion: but that it is a ſummary and abridgment of all that Moſes in the law, and the ſucceeding prophets, have laid down relative to our duty to our neighbour; and that all the particular precepts and directions they have given with regard to ſocial duties, are compriſed and virtually implied in this one general rule; a rule which all the divine revelations to mankind, in the law and the prophets, tended ultimately to eſtabliſh.

And in order to enforce the obſervance of this rule among the different ranks and orders of men, the higheſt, as well as the loweſt, let it be conſidered, that how wide ſoever the diſtance may appear, which birth, fortune, or ſtation, may have made between one perſon and another; however different and unequal the lots aſſigned

ed us; yet that these distinctions are merely adventitious and accidental; that the whole race of mankind are of one stock, derived from the same common original, the workmanship of the same hands, formed with the same immortal souls, impressed with the same divine image, and alike related to God, the equal Father of all; and that as all men are by nature thus equal, they are alike subject to every moral obligation, and have all an equal right to the same equitable treatment.

Let it be also further considered, how uncertain and precarious is the possession of those distinctions which elevate one person above another; and how often those who are by nature equal, are reduced to an equality of condition. What security have the great and the fortunate, that they shall not one day be numbered among the least and lowest of mankind? Such is the contingency, such the fluctuation, of all human affairs; so many surprising revolutions often happen, and the wheel turns sometimes so quickly round, that it is

very

very poffible that to-morrow's fun may find him eating the bread of affliction, who has hitherto fared fumptuoufly every day. This uncertainty may furnifh a prudential motive, to conduct ourfelves with that equity and benevolence to our fellow-creatures in one ftation of life, which we would defire and expect from them in another.

They therefore to whom Heaven has with a more liberal hand diftributed the talents of wifdom, wealth, or power, fhould be wifely merciful; and employ their wifdom in informing the ignorant, their wealth in relieving the indigent, their power in protecting the injured;— left themfelves fhould poffibly be one day reduced to fupplicate in vain that affiftance, protection, or relief, which they now refufe to others. Prudence, as well as religion, bids all perfons, by an honeft and humane behaviour, to make provifion for good ufage from others, which they may poffibly ftand in need of, and which fuch a behaviour would give them a right to expect.

III. I proceed, in the last place, to observe the utility and excellence of the rule prescribed in the text. Which may appear, first, in its being well adapted to general use, and suited to all capacities.—It is as easy and obvious to common understandings, as to the most penetrating discernment. Its evidence depends not on an accurate deduction of arguments; it is no laboured conclusion drawn from a long chain of intricate reasoning, to which few have capacity or inclination to attend; but it carries light and conviction along with it, and can hardly be misapprehended. Most other rules of conduct are more complex; have in them some obscurity; and, by being involved in a variety of circumstances, may require attention and discernment to determine when and to what degree they are obligatory: but the simplicity of this rule renders the application of it intelligible to all. Let us but
consult

consult this oracle, and the way lies plain before us; the rule of righteousness is clear as the light, and the measure of just dealings as the noon-day.

Another instance of the utility of this precept is, that it is applicable to all circumstances; is a full, adequate, and complete rule of behaviour. Our SAVIOUR was the first who taught this comprehensive aphorism worthy of a divine teacher; which comprises in it the whole duty of man to man, and is of more avail in the commerce of life, than all the lectures of Heathen moralists. It may direct our whole social conduct; so that as no emergency can be so sudden as not to allow time to have recourse to it, so no case can happen in which it will not determine. It will inform us what is due, on every occasion, and in all circumstances, to superiors, equals, or inferiors. It is as applicable to lesser matters of civility and decency, as to more consequential, moral duties; and extends to all ranks and denominations of men,—to the rich and the poor, the prosperous and unfortunate, the master

master and the servant, the monarch and the subject. If in all our intercourse with others, we invert the case, and place ourselves in our neighbour's situation, and consider him in our's,—our own heart will always be casuist enough to point out and prescribe a right and proper conduct.

Let us then attend to this important and comprehensive rule of behaviour, and keep it ever in view, that we may form our whole conduct by it; that we may check the impulses of unfriendly passions, correct the partiality of self-love, and act on all occasions as reason and equity direct. Were but this one precept duly attended to, and adopted into general practice, how would it change the scene of human life! what large additions would it make to the public happiness! It would introduce so much peace, and order, and harmony, and virtue into the world, as would render it the image of heaven, or make it like itself at its creation, when every thing was pronounced *good*. We should then see no injustice, and hear *no complaining in our streets*.

Injuries

Injuries and oppreſſions would not then invade the quiet of private life; nor would ambitious power violate the right of nations, nor deviſe barbarous arts of propagating ruin and extending deſolation through the world. In every ſtation, men, by acting up to their reſpective obligations, and by maintaining a commerce of mutual good offices, would concur in fixing and eſtabliſhing the general happineſs of mankind upon the moſt ſolid baſis,—that of univerſal virtue.

Let it alſo be remembered, that we muſt all one day appear at the awful tribunal of Heaven, to render an account of our obedience to this law; where the JUDGE of the whole earth will reward every man according to his works, and act by us as we have done to each other. With the upright man, HE will ſhow himſelf upright. If we have forgiven others their treſpaſſes, HE will forgive ours; if we have had compaſſion on our fellow-ſervants, HE will have compaſſion upon us. If, then, we would act as reaſonable beings;

ings; if we would attend to what is not only the substance of the law and the prophets, but the spirit of the gospel; if we desire to add to the common happiness of mankind in this world, or to secure our own in the next;—we must inscribe this short abstract of duty upon our hearts, in order to be faithfully copied out into our life and manners,—*Whatsoever ye would that men should do unto you, do ye even so to them.*

SERMON XVII.

Sins of Infirmity and Presumption.

PSAL. xix. 12, 13.

Who can tell how oft he offendeth? O cleanse thou me from my secret faults. Keep thy servant also from presumptuous sins, lest they get the dominion over me: so shall I be undefiled, and innocent from the great offence.

MANKIND are apt to form various misapprehensions concerning the degrees of malignity and guilt in different sins; and are inclined often to extenuate, sometimes to aggravate, their failings too much. Some pious persons, desirous to walk in all the commandments of GOD blameless, and to approach as near as may be to religious perfection,—studious

studious to please, and afraid to offend, their MAKER,—are apt to pass too severe a sentence upon themselves for the mere slips of infirmity, and their fears magnify errors or inadvertencies into transgressions and crimes. Others there are, (and they by far the most numerous), who, though they act, in many instances, in plain and direct opposition to the laws of religion; yet, with a dangerous partiality or self-deception, persuade themselves, that theirs are only the lapses of natural infirmity, the unavoidable effects of human frailty,—fit objects of compassion rather than of justice, and entitled to an easy and certain forgiveness.

So indulgent, generally, are mankind to their own faults, and such the prepossession in their own favour,—that there are few sins so black and flagitious, few so presumptuous and of so deep a dye, but the offender will, from partial reasoning, excuse to himself under the pretext of Infirmity, and consider them only as slight and venial failings. To prevent, therefore, this dangerous self-deception on the one hand, and a groundless self-condemnation on the other; that we may neither presume ourselves to be better, nor apprehend we are worse, than we are; it may be proper to mark the distinction between sins of Infirmity and sins of Presumption; the former not imputable to us as Crimes, the latter not to be forgiven without Repentance.

I shall therefore observe, 1*st*, What failures in our conduct are to be considered as sins of Infirmity; and, 2*dly*, What actions deserve the severer appellation of *presumptuous sins*.

I. Let us observe what deviations from the divine laws are to be considered as sins of Infirmity.

These are, first, such as proceed from some ignorance or error that is involuntary, and, in a moral construction, unavoidable. Where failings are occasioned by ignorance strictly and absolutely invincible, *i. e.* from a natural incapacity, or from an absolute want of sufficient means of information, there they can have no
degree

degree of criminality in them; where they are the consequences of determined and wilful ignorance, they are highly sinful.

But where they proceed from some error that is, in a moral construction, unavoidable,—that is, such error as, all circumstances considered, we could not reasonably be expected to escape; or such as we are naturally, and almost inevitably, led into by the influence of education or example; from the weakness of our intellectual faculties, or the want of light necessary to assist us in forming a right judgment; or from prejudices which darken our understanding, or from difficulties and obscurities in things themselves;—while errors arise almost necessarily from such causes, these will be admitted, we may hope, as a good plea at the merciful tribunal of Heaven.

Ignorance that is not careless, affected, or voluntary, being a misfortune, not a fault, will most certainly render us fit objects of divine compassion, and not of indignation. This our blessed Lord himself,

self, upon the cross, pleaded in extenuation of the worst of crimes: *Father, forgive them; for they know not what they do.* And to this St Paul attributes his own forgiveness: *I obtained mercy*, says he, *because I did it ignorantly, in unbelief.*

But it is to be observed, that in glaring crimes, and plain transgressions of the divine laws, inevitable ignorance cannot be pleaded; for of our great moral obligations we are sufficiently informed, both by the light of Nature and of Revelation. The principal laws of GOD are written with great perspicuity, both in our hearts and in the gospel; and the most important lines of duty are obvious and legible to every eye. The plea of ignorance can be admitted so far only as that ignorance is inevitable, and not the effect of a dishonest disposition or voluntary neglect.

2*dly*, Those failings, or violations of the divine laws, are to be reputed sins of infirmity, into which we are betrayed by inadvertence or surprise,—though this surprise may not be strictly and absolutely ly unavoidable, but such as, considering the various circumstances of human life, the frequent inattention of our minds, and the sudden impression of objects upon them, cannot always be avoided, even by the most vigilant and attentive. Of this kind are the lesser, unpremeditated irregularities of passion, inconsiderate expressions, inclinations in some measure criminal, that come uninvited into the mind, and proceed not indeed to action, but yet are received and entertained with too much approbation. These, and other similar failings, are incident to the wisest and best; upon which account the Psalmist says, *Who can tell how oft he offendeth?* and the Apostle observes, that *if we say we have no sin, we deceive ourselves, and the truth is not in us.*

II. Having thus observed some general marks or characters of what are properly and truly sins of Infirmity, I shall next proceed to show what actions deserve the severer appellation of *presumptuous sins.*

1st, Those are presumptuous sins which are

are committed againſt light and knowledge. The nature of ſin conſiſts in a voluntary departure from the rule of our duty, in ſuffering ourſelves to be ſeduced by ſome intereſt or paſſion, to act contrary to the law of God, whether communicated by reaſon or revelation. And the nature and eſſence of preſumptuous ſin conſiſts in acting againſt our own convictions, in doing what at the very inſtant of commiſſion we know and acknowledge to be ſinful. It is this conſciouſneſs, this conviction, which renders the action highly criminal, and juſtly puniſhable by a wiſe and righteous Governor. And though there may be great diſtinctions, and various extenuations, as well as aggravations, of ſuch offences; yet every action of this kind is in ſome degree a preſumptuous ſin, committed in avowed oppoſition to God and his authority.

2*dly*, They alſo may be ſaid to ſin preſumptuouſly, who ſin from wilful inattention and ignorance; who have frequent opportunities of having the doctrines and
duties

duties of religion laid before them, and of being informed, or reminded, of its obligations,—but wilfully refuse their attention, and shun opportunities of information. Our CREATOR has made us intellectual beings, capable of examining and distinguishing good and evil, truth and falsehood; and may, doubtless, with justice, demand from us a conduct suitable to those advantages. This duty is still heightened by the revealed assistances he vouchsafes, and the providential means of improvement he puts in our power. These are talents for which we justly stand accountable to the all-gracious DONOR; and the neglect of them cannot but be wrong in itself, and highly offensive to HIM. All voluntary error must therefore be criminal; criminal in the same degree as it is voluntary; and the guilt or malignity of it is in proportion to the power of avoiding it.

Some persons may be weak enough to prefer darkness to light, when they are determined that their deeds shall be evil; may choose to avoid information and instruction,

struction, when they are resolved to persist in their vices; and may imagine that their ignorance of duty will extenuate their transgression of it. But such ignorance, proceeding not from an inability to find out their duty, but from a resolution not to seek it—from a corrupt heart, and dishonest disposition,—has in it all the essence and guilt of sin. We may affirm, that not they only are presumptuous sinners, who at the very instant of perpetrating wickedness act in conscious opposition to the will of Heaven; but that they also are such, who are voluntarily negligent and remiss in their inquiries after GOD's will; and choose rather to be ignorant than informed of the rules he has laid down,—from a suspicion, that those rules might interrupt or disturb them in their criminal pursuits, and from a resolution to avoid and guard against such interruption and disturbance.

3*dly*, As to commit an action against our own convictions of its guilt, is the highest aggravation of sin; so our consent to an action, the lawfulness of which, after deliberate confideration, appears fufpicious and doubtful, is in a lower degree a prefumptuous fin alfo; becaufe it is voluntarily and knowingly complying with what we have reafon to apprehend may be criminal in itfelf, and difpleafing to GOD. Though the merciful Author of our being is not extreme to mark what is done amifs by his creatures; though he makes gracious allowances for defects, and compaffionates our frailties; yet purity of intention, an honeft and good heart, is what he ftrictly requires as the indifpenfable condition of his favour. And this purity of intention, this goodnefs of heart, will fhow itfelf in all cafes where the lawfulnefs of an action is doubtful, by adhering to that fide where our integrity will be moft fecure, and by avoiding doubtful and fufpected, as much as evident and certain guilt.

Having thus marked the general characters of fuch actions as deferve the fevere appellation of *prefumptuous fins*, I fhall only obferve farther, that of prefumptuous finners there are different ranks and degrees, which

which it may not be improper briefly to mention.

In the lowest and least culpable degree are they who preserve in their minds a just sense of the obligations of religion, and form the general course of their lives by its rules, and have virtue enough to resist frequent solicitations to guilt; but yet on some occasions, by the force of particular temptations, suffer themselves to be seduced against their own convictions. Such persons are, in those particular instances, presumptuous sinners; though, upon the whole, they deserve not the appellation of *wicked*,—as their general behaviour has been right, and conformable to the precepts of virtue. Yet, as they have done what they ought not to have done, and have in some instances acted contrary to the laws of GOD, and the acknowledgements of their own hearts,—repentance and amendment are certainly necessary in order to obtain forgiveness.

In the next and more guilty rank of presumptuous sinners, are to be placed those who

who have some sense of duty, and some intention of observing it; but yet their sense of duty is not vigorous and effectual enough to prevent their compliance with almost every temptation that offers to corrupt them. On every trial, whenever their religious integrity is put to the test, and on the only occasions wherein they can evidence their sincerity, they give proofs only of the feebleness of their resolution, and of their ineffectual sense of religious principles, which, whenever seducements invite, they are ready to renounce.

In the highest and most criminal class of sinners, are those who form deliberate schemes of guilt; who premeditate and project plans of wickedness; and, without being led into temptation, become their own tempters, and search about for opportunities of iniquity, determined to lay hold on those that offer. To such it will be of little consequence, with regard to their guilt, whether they find, or not, the opportunities they seek. For in the eye of Heaven, and of Justice, guilt lies in the
intention

intention of guilt. He who determines to commit a crime when occaſion offers, commits it in his heart; and his previous deliberation greatly adds to the malignity of his ſin. Men, indeed, cannot penetrate the inward intention; human juſtice can take no cogniſance of the heart, and can judge of guilt only by appearances: but the all-ſeeing eye of God diſcerns the inward intention much better than we can ſee the outward action,—and He judges the heart.

May what has been now offered, prevail with us to enter into a ſerious examination of ourſelves, and make a ſtrict inſpection into our lives and manners. Have we been guilty of ſins of infirmity, (as what man is he that liveth and ſinneth not?) let us not neglect to implore pardon and forgiveneſs; and to this end, the repentance we exerciſe in our uſual devotions ſhould ſeem to ſuffice. Sins of infirmity are what the Pſalmiſt calls ſecret ſins; ſuch as cannot all be particularly noted, nor remembered; and cannot therefore demand a particular, but only a general, repentance.

ance. But with regard to prefumptuous fins, fins deliberately committed, committed againſt the conviction of our own heart and confcience, which are ever recurring to the mind, and which we cannot, if we would, forget,—the deepeſt contrition of foul, and a particular application to the throne of Mercy, are doubtlefs abfolutely required.

To avoid, as much as may be, all fin, whether of Infirmity or Prefumption,—let us, to the moſt vigilant attention to our ways, add our conſtant fupplications to GOD for his aſſiſting grace; and let each of us addrefs him in the words of the Pfalmiſt,—*Who can tell how oft he offendeth? O cleanfe thou me from my fecret faults. Keep thy fervant alfo from prefumptuous fins, left they get the dominion over me: fo fhall I be undefiled and innocent from the great offence.*

SERMON XVIII.

On the Resurrection.

1 Cor. vi. 14.

God hath both raised up the Lord, and will also raise us up by his own power.

THE prospect beyond this life, and the state and condition of man after his descent into the grave and the dissolution of the body, has been a speculation which has amused the ignorant, and perplexed the wise, in all ages of the world. Before the revelation of the Gospel, the future existence of human nature was a disputable problem; the disquisitions of philosophers terminated only in diffident expectations; and their conclusions were such as their wishes, rather than conviction, led them to believe.

Beyond the visible boundary of death, what may be our doom; whither we shall be conveyed; through what scenes we are to pass, or for what duration we may exist; whether we shall be capable of sensation when divested of the body; what the specific nature of the enjoyments allotted us; what capacities and powers we may possess, or what we have to hope or fear,—no human sagacity or art could ever discover. It was all a region of uncertainty, a land of darkness, from whence no departed spirit had ever returned to bring information. Of the existence of this state the heathen world were doubtful. One of the poets of antiquity * pathetically complains, that while the luminaries of heaven, the sun and stars, set and rise again; yet man, when he descends into the grave, sinks down into perpetual night, and sets, never to rise:—and that

* Moschus.

while the vegetable race, the plants and flowers of the field, fade and decay, and obtain a kind of resurrection in the spring; yet the best of human beings wither and perish, without any prospect or hope of restoration to life.

But the Christian Revelation has dissipated the uncertainties with regard to a future state; and, by the resurrection of CHRIST from the dead, hath given us the inestimable assurance, that the grave does not put a period to our being; that the soul is not to sleep in perpetual night; that the end of life is but the beginning of immortality, and death no other than a new birth to another state of existence.

As the resurrection of our blessed LORD is the surest foundation of our future hopes, I shall observe, 1*st*, The credibility of that fact; and, 2*dly*, The consequent certainty of our own resurrection.

I. Let us observe the credibility of the resurrection of our blessed LORD. As his resurrection was an event in its nature astonishing, and important in its consequences,

quences, it should seem to have been the care of the Supreme Wisdom to establish the credibility of it upon the firmest foundation. It is not necessary to collect the whole accumulative evidence of our Lord's resurrection, nor minutely to detail all the various circumstances that concur to illustrate and confirm the truth of it. It may suffice to mention, that our Lord, after he arose from the dead, appeared to his disciples with this particular view, that they might testify this fact, and be proper and unexceptionable witnesses of it; that he continued forty days showing himself alive after his passion, by many infallible proofs; and after several private appearances to his apostles, was seen of above five hundred brethren at once.

The apostles, we may observe, cannot be charged with credulity in the article of our Lord's resurrection. When he was betrayed, they all forsook him and fled; they were offended at the ignominy of his crucifixion; and all their hopes and expectations seem to have expired with their MASTER upon the crofs. The firft accounts of his refurrection met with little credit among them; and when he appeared to the apoftles affembled together, they were terrified, fuppofing him to be a Spirit.

True it is, our LORD fhowed himfelf not openly to all the people, but to witneffes chofen before of GOD; the reafon of which might be (if we may be permitted to affign the reafons of the divine conduct), that GOD does not in any inftance do all that he has power to do, but fo much only as to his wifdom appears right and expedient. He employs fuch means only as are in their nature fitted to produce conviction, when attended to with an upright and honeft heart. That the Divine BEING may awake all our faculties, and open our underftanding, fo as to compel an admiffion of thofe truths he is pleafed to reveal,—and may convert every unbeliever, in the fame miraculous and irrefiftible manner as he did St Paul,—is certain and uncontefted: but it is not the ufual method

method of his providence. He leaves us generally to the application of our intellectual powers, and to that freedom of will which can alone conftitute the merit of religious faith or practice. The witneffes of our LORD's refurrection were as numerous as the nature of the fact required, and fuch as were moft capable of judging of the identity of his perfon.

When they afferted his refurrection, they afferted a fact in which there was no room for deception. They well knew his perfon, his features, his manner; were admitted to familiar converfe, that they might be fure they were not deceived by any aërial phantom or illufive appearance.

And as it is impoffible they fhould be themfelves deceived, it is equally incredible that they fhould attempt an impofition on the world. For that they fhould, in direct oppofition to their own native prejudices and evident interefts,—without any lucrative views in this world, without any profpect of reward in the next,—perfift to death in the atteftation of what they knew to be a falsehood; and, for the sake of one who had deceived them, form a deliberate concerted plan to expose themselves to the severest sufferings and tortures, to which all men have naturally an unsurmountable aversion,—is a supposition that cannot be admitted with the least appearance of reason. For, is it credible, that they could extinguish in themselves all the hopes and fears, the passions, affections, and feelings, of human nature? that they could divest themselves of the principle of self-preservation? that they could enter, as it were, into a conspiracy against their own ease, interest, and reputation? throw off all regard to the happiness or enjoyment of life, all care even for their own quiet and security? And for what? to meet poverty and persecution, reproach and contempt, bonds and imprisonments, sufferings and death, without any view of interest present or future? To this they could have no conceivable temptation or inducement, according to all the principles or motives that are known to influence or operate upon

the

Ser. 18. *On the Resurrection.* 263

the human mind. On the contrary, on the suppofition of Christ's not being rifen, they muft have been fenfible that he was a deceiver; that the promifes and predictions with which he had amufed them, had failed; and that from him, confequently, they could have no grounds of hope either here or hereafter.

In fhort, that a number of perfons of found underftanding, and honeft characters, fhould unanimoufly combine to atteft and fupport a falfehood, in oppofition to all their interefts and prejudices,—to every principle that can be fuppofed to influence human actions, and at the hazard of every thing valuable and dear to men,—is abfolutely unaccountable; and would be as aftonifhing, and as ftrictly miraculous, as any interruption or violation of the common courfe of nature.

If we confider, further, the atteftation of Heaven to the veracity of the apoftles, expreffed in the power conferred on them of performing miracles, fpeaking in the language of all nations, and of healing

R 4 all

all manner of diseases; a testimony so circumstanced must be concluded to carry in it all the evidence that any distant fact can possibly be capable of; and far superior to the proof of any other fact recorded in ancient history. No single fact in all history is either supported by such unexceptionable witnesses, or comes to us confirmed with such collateral and subsequent evidence. We may be assured, therefore, that *God hath raised up the Lord, and will therefore raise up us also by his own power.* ——Which leads me,

II. To inquire into the certainty of our own resurrection. Before life and immortality were brought to light by the Gospel, human nature could ill sustain the melancholy reflection that its prospect might be closed, and its existence determined in the grave; and that the evening of life might be succeeded by a long, eternal night. The vulgar, therefore, supported themselves with fictions, the wise with uncertain hopes and conjectures, of the soul's immortality. But that the body should return from corruption

ruption to a reunion with the foul, was not expected by the wifeft. The Jews, it is true, might have fome conception of this, from the tranflation of Enoch and Elijah to heaven in their bodies; and from Job's declaration of his affurance, that in his flefh he fhould fee GOD. And indeed, as our CREATOR has thought fit, in our prefent ftate, to unite the foul to a corporeal fubftance, this fhould feem to intimate, that the nature of the foul is fuch, that a body fuited to the ftate of its future exiftence may be requifite to the due exertion of its powers, and that confequently there may be a refurrection of the body. But the clear difcovery of this important truth was referved for the Author and Finifher of our Faith. We are now aflured, that *the hour is coming, when all that are in the grave fhall hear the voice of the Son of man, and fhall come forth.*

The refurrection of our LORD is an atteftation from heaven, that, during his refidence upon earth, he neither acted, promifed, nor taught, but in conformity to the

the will of God, with whose authority he declared himself to be invested. And the reason of this is clear: Because it is utterly irreconcileable with those ideas of the divine attributes, which must direct us in all our religious inquiries; and impossible therefore, to conceive, that the God of truth would either decree or permit an evidence of so high a nature to be given to any person who had assumed a false character in his name, or had taught, or acted, under that character, in a manner not agreeable to his will.

If, therefore, Christ predicted and affirmed that he would raise the dead; and, in proof of his assertion, subdued the powers of death, and ascended from the grave; there can be no room to doubt, that what he hath accomplished in his own person, he will also fulfil in us. If he verified his prediction to the Jews, *Destroy this temple, and in three days I will build it up;* if he restored the temple of his own body, doubtless he can also rebuild these earthly tenements of ours. He who raised

fed up Jesus from the dead, can also quicken our mortal bodies; and in order to give us an assurance that he will raise us up, the resurrection of Christ was made the promise and pledge of the resurrection of the whole human species.

Nor let it be thought a thing incredible, that God should raise the dead. For tho' the materials of our bodies should be disunited and dissolved, mingled with dust, or evaporated into air, dissipated and dispersed over the whole face of nature; yet it is infinitely easy to him, to whose all-comprehensive mind all objects are at once minutely and distinctly presented, to recal, collect, and arrange, every atom, if needful. Every the smallest particle of matter, though lost and imperceptible to us, is yet pursued by his all-seeing eye through all its changes, and by his hand guided and conducted in its progress in all its various stations. He who formed man from dust, can questionless re-animate the same dust. He who gave life, can restore it; can re-organise the scattered atoms, if needful,

needful, and difpofe them in the fame order as before.

How far indeed our bodies fhall be formed of precifely the fame portions of matter they confifted of at the time of their diffolution, or at any other period of their being, is a point that has not been revealed, and cannot be determined. It is a queftion of no moral import, fo long as the mind is the fame; which is all that concerns us. It may fuffice to all the purpofes of religion to be informed, that though *we lie down in difhonour, we fhall be raifed in glory*; and that *our Saviour Chrift will change thefe bodies, that they may be like unto his glorious body, according to the mighty power whereby he is able to fubdue all things to himfelf.*

What has been obferved may fuggeft the following reflections.

1ſt, If our bleſſed LORD, by his refurrection from the dead, has given us ſtronger aſſurances than ever the world had before of a future exiſtence,—this may reconcile us to death, and difarm that laſt adverſary

versary of his terrors. It will moderate and compose our fears, when we reflect, that though it is appointed unto men to die;—though the vital union between soul and body must one day be dissolved, and we must descend into the dark mansions of death:—yet that we are not to be for ever imprisoned in those mansions, not to be extinguished in the grave: that death translates us to a happier state of being: that the separation of the soul and body is only for a time; and that, too, in order to a more perfect union, which shall never be dissolved. All beyond the grave is no longer an unknown region, a land of darkness, or a state of oblivion, where all our thoughts perish. We may now consider death, not only as a secure sanctuary, a safe retreat from all the fears and pains, the labours and sorrows of life,—but as the gate to immortality, the passage to glory, the avenue to heaven. We are now assured, that we shall go whither our Saviour and Redeemer is gone before us; and that where he is we shall be also.

2dly,

2dly, If the awful day is approaching when *thefe corruptible bodies fhall put on incorruption, and thefe mortal fhall put on immortality*; when the grave fhall reftore its afhes, and the fea give up her dead;—how careful ought we to be, fo to conduct ourfelves in this life, that we may be able to look beyond it without terror or apprehenfion; that we may be prepared to meet our REDEEMER and JUDGE, and may have hope in that decifive hour which determines our everlafting ftate. I doubt not but all here prefent have hopes, with St Paul, that there will be a refurrection both of the juft and the unjuft: May we all, with him, refolve to exercife ourfelves, therefore, to have always a confcience void of offence towards GOD and towards man.

Laftly, Let us reflect what bleffing and praife are due, how much we owe to the mercies of the GOD and FATHER of our Lord JESUS CHRIST, whofe kind providence guards and protects us in life; forfakes us not even in death; and has, in the refurrection of his SON, given us a
pledge

pledge and affurance of a future ftate of immortal happinefs. O may it be our firft, our daily and habitual care, to render ourfelves fit objects of his favour, and not unworthy of fuch happinefs,—by every expreffion of pious obedience; by a facred attention to every duty, every injunction of the SAVIOUR of mankind, who lived and died, and rofe again, for us; that in the laft day, when he fhall come again in his glorious Majefty to judge the world, we may be favoured with his approbation, and be deemed worthy to enter into life eternal!

SERMON XIX.

On Peace.

Rom. xii. 18.

If it be possible, as much as lieth in you, live peaceably with all men.

WHENEVER we look abroad into the world, and with a serious eye survey and contemplate the state and condition of human nature, we cannot, without the most painful impressions, reflect, how much human life is embittered, and its numerous afflictions multiplied and aggravated, by the cruel addition of the various calamities which mankind inflict on each other:—calamities, not derived from

the

the neceffary condition of our being, not from any immutable law of nature, not inflicted by Providence; but voluntarily introduced by our own malignant paffions, in oppofition to the monitions and precepts of our CREATOR.

If mankind would univerfally conform to the original plan of the great AUTHOR of their being, and fteadily purfue thofe paths of virtue and benevolence which he has pointed out, and in which he has inftructed them to walk; if they would uniformly act on the principles of religion, and become an holy fraternity, and every man confider himfelf as brother to every man;—how great an abatement might be made in the forrows and miferies of human life! how happily improved would be the ftate of mankind! how joyful and pleafant to affociate and dwell together, like brethren, in unity! Meeknefs, moderation, and equity, would then guard the fecurity of individuals; and juftice, benevolence, mercy, and other focial virtues, would infure the public tranquillity.

quillity. All the most desirable advantages of civil life would be secured, and the natural effect of universal righteousness would be universal peace. All the virtues would combine in a happy confederacy to promote the peace and tranquillity of human nature, and to make earth resemble heaven in happiness as in goodness.

The Gospel is one continued lesson of all the virtues conducive to this end; and in almost every page instructs us to be placable and meek, candid and peaceful, benevolent and compassionate. But how widely different from the precepts of Christianity are the manners of many who assume the name of Christians! instead of cherishing friendly dispositions, and exerting themselves in kind offices, how common is it to see them seize every opportunity of fomenting discord, of offering or returning injuries, and of making that the entertainment of the heart that ought to be most disgustful to it.

In this discourse I shall consider the duty recommended in the text; and shall offer some

some considerations to engage your observance of it.

I. In order, then, to promote or preserve the amicable and pacific spirit of unity recommended in the text, it ought to be our habitual endeavour, to suppress or restrict all those inclinations or passions which would inflame our sense of injuries; and cherish all such sentiments and considerations as may recommend mildness, moderation, and harmony. We must be slow to take, and careful not to give, offence. We must not take disgust where no occasion is given; and where a slight one is offered, we must make no difficulty to overlook it. We must not suffer our resentment to rise without a cause, nor allow it to be violent and intemperate even with one. And though this may lay us under a necessity of sometimes departing from our right, and of making concessions which strict justice might not demand; yet, nevertheless, a compliance is required from all who would live up to their duty, and conform to the pacific precepts of our divine Religion.

Calmness, indeed, and moderation, in cases where injuries wound, and wrongs irritate; where nature prompts, and fashion and custom seem in some measure to demand and to justify resentment,—are, it must be acknowledged, no easy task. To bless the tongue that calumniates, or the hand that smites us, is a severe restraint to our passions, a hard injunction to corrupt nature. But it is to be considered, that in such cases we are not to listen to our passions, but to duty; we are not to consult fashion, custom, or inclination, but religion. The precepts of the Gospel equally forbid the offering, or returning, of a wrong. *Bless them that curse you,* says our blessed Lord; *pray for them which despitefully use you.*

Many other precepts there are of the same import, enjoined by the authority of our Lord, and enforced by his example; which ought therefore to prevail with us, not to listen to the suggestions of pride, passion,

passion, custom, or any principle of false honour, which would dissuade us from the pacific virtues.

Some there are who would charge the violation of the duty in the text solely upon the first aggressors; and think it may be lawful to return, though not to offer, an injury. But how vain were it to urge this duty, if so easy an evasion were left to malice and revenge? how vain to enjoin peace and union, if so colourable a pretext were admitted for strife and dissension? For there are few that will acknowledge, or perhaps can persuade themselves, that their anger is unreasonable, and without a just foundation. Even when, in their own opinion, their wrongs have received satisfaction; when their passions are cooled by reflection, and time has laid their resentment asleep; yet they will be apt, in general, to justify it; though they may possibly be ingenuous enough to confess, that it may have been carried too far. Some plead for a liberty of resenting and retaliating injuries which have been severe and oppressive;

oppressive; though they are willing to censure and condemn that resentment which rises upon trivial occasions or imaginary wrongs. But since imaginary wrongs often make as deep a wound, and are as painful, as real ones, and are considered as such; and as every man assumes a privilege to judge for himself, and to feel the weight of his own wrongs,—every man would be apt to interpret this distinction in his own favour.

Besides, where is the difficulty, or where the virtue, of preserving our temper, or suppressing our resentment, where no extraordinary occasions occur to disconcert or disquiet us? The test of our virtue is, when others can be so far forgetful of themselves and their duty, as to offend or injure us without cause. If, upon such occasions, we can forgive offences, and curb revenge, and forbear repaying evil with evil,—such behaviour will show, that we pay a just regard to the precepts and authority of Religion.

II. To engage our attention to this duty, it

it might be sufficient to observe, that it is the best preservative of our own quiet and tranquillity, which can never dwell in the same bosom with anger, malice, and resentment. These are painful passions, that distort the mind, and force it into the most uneasy postures. But to bear no ill-will, to be kindly affectioned, to be in friendship and at peace with the world and with ourselves,—is the most desirable condition, the pleasantest situation, the easiest attitude of the soul. Happy the man, happy in himself, and amiable in the eye of the world, who thus conducts himself; whose habitual object it is to contribute to the tranquillity, the satisfaction, the happiness, of all with whom he has connection or intercourse; who regards others with the same eye of tenderness with which he wishes to be regarded by them; is humble, humane, and peaceful; grants no indulgence to unfriendly passions, but is always disposed to cherish and exert kind affections, and to extend them to his friends, his neighbours, and all mankind.

On the other hand, he who is employed in meditating and projecting schemes of revenge, can have no quiet, no self-enjoyment, no peace of mind; but must be unhappy, both when he forms his plan of revenge, and carries it into execution, and afterwards reflects upon it. Providence has appointed, that both the devising of mischief, and the reflection upon it afterwards, shall be vexatious and painful; and has wisely ordained, that whoever meditates against the peace of another, shall in the design lose his own. A transient gleam of pleasure may result from accomplishing our vindictive projects; but to a reasonable, considerate mind, forbearance, patience, and forgiveness, will afford a much more amiable and permanent satisfaction. The monuments of our kindness are objects that we always with pleasure view and contemplate; but nothing appears with more terror to our cool reflections, than the retrospect of a life marked with acts of malice, cruelty, and revenge.

Discord and dissension are, in Scripture, condemned,

condemned, sometimes on account of the unhappy consequences they produce, at other times on account of the evil principles from which they proceed. *From whence come wars and fightings among you?* says the Apostle; whence all those disaffections and enmities that divide mankind? *Come they not hence, even from your lusts?* from intemperate and ungoverned passions? These, upon inquiry, will appear to be the true source of divisions. The avarice of the covetous, *e. g.* and the insolence of the proud, can hardly fail to involve them in contentions. Does any one interfere with the interest of the former, or offend the vanity of the latter; they are immediately in arms, and consider all as their enemies who stand in the way of their favourite pursuit. So also the resentful man always finds fuel for resentment in the behaviour of others; and the malice of the envious makes him averse to every one whose situation he supposes to be happier than his own.

If these be the grounds and occasions of dissensions, they may point out the means
of

of preserving unity and peace. To this end, let not passion dictate to us the opinion we form of others: let us be candid and equitable in our judgments: let us make allowances for temper and infirmity, and not impute the mistakes of inadvertence to malice and deliberate design. Impossible it often is to penetrate into all the circumstances which determine the nature of actions. Their outward appearances may lie before us: but their internal springs, the hidden purposes, the secret intentions, and true motives of the heart, we cannot discern; and after all our inquiries, we must sit down with conjectures only. If, then, we can judge only by appearances, which are often fallacious; if the heart of man is inscrutable, except to HIM that made it,—we should permit candour and charity to plead in behalf of others, and suggest the most favourable construction of their actions. Such a conduct would not only be a proof of our inclination to unity and peace, but would in some measure obtain its end, as it would prevent

prevent us from being too precipitate in condemning others, from yielding to the first impulses of passion; it would give time to reason and reflection to correct the wrong impressions of a hasty surmise, and thus cut off many occasions of dissension.

Another common source of dissension is Pride, or a too high estimation of our rank, merit, or talents; and, what naturally accompanies it, too contemptuous ideas of others. This turn of mind renders the proud man too assuming; prompts him to require more attention than others think he has a just claim to; and exposes him to what he considers as indignities and insults; which he estimates always in proportion to the high value he sets upon himself, and the low opinion he forms of others. Such occasions of dissension we should prevent, if we could be prevailed on not to think more highly of ourselves than we ought to think. We view ourselves with partial eyes, and are very improper judges of our own merits or defects; it is common to magnify the former, and diminish the latter. Accurately

to

to discern, and impartially to decide upon them, requires a mind more disengaged from the prejudices and prepossessions we naturally form in our own favour, than generally falls to the share of mankind. To judge with precision of our own merit, is no easy task; but to presume upon too high an opinion of it, is evidently a weakness. Were we able to correct this one weakness, we should become more humble, moderate, and peaceful; we should not be disconcerted at every neglect of our presumed merit, nor be at variance with those who differed from us in the estimate we had made of ourselves.

Thus, by judging of ourselves with humility, and of others with candour, we may obviate many occasions of discord and contention, and may preserve and promote harmony and peace: a duty to which, both as men and Christians, we ought to be attentive; for both wisdom and religion, prudence and duty, concur in their exhortations to us, to live peaceably with all men, and to endeavour, as much as lieth in us, to dwell together, like brethren, in unity.

SERMON XX.

On Contentment.

1 Tim. vi. 6.

Godliness with contentment is great gain.

THOUGH nothing is more certain, than that all earthly enjoyments are defective, and that neither nature nor Providence will permit us to pass through life without a portion of that trouble to which we are born; yet equally certain it is, that we often abridge those enjoyments, and add to that trouble, by habituating ourselves to contemplate the dark side only of our condition; by overlooking or underrating what is in our power, pointing our view to objects out of our reach; and by an opinion, which observation could not fail to refute, that the happiness of life consisteth in the abundance we possess.

To prevent the unhappiness consequent on this turn of mind, the duty of Contentment recommended in the text is well worthy of our attention, and is of all others the most essential to our quiet. Other duties are enjoined, that we may be virtuous and good: Contentment is prescribed to make us happy,—happy as our state will permit; to supply the deficiencies that must occur; to be a substitute for enjoyments that will be always wanting. Without this virtue, no condition of life can be happy; and with it, none can be wretched.

In order, then, to form our minds to an acquiescence in that state, whatever it be, wherein the Supreme Disposer of all things has placed us; let it be observed, that as, by the original plan and appointment of the Creator, the talents, stations,

tions, and powers, of mankind, are infinitely diverfified, hence muft neceffarily arife various fubordinations, various gradations of pre-eminence and fuperiority in fome, and of dependence and fubjection in others. And it may hence be inferred, that fuch diverfity appeared to the Supreme Wifdom to be moft conducive to the end he had in view,—the general good and well-being of his creatures: for certain it is, that in his government of the world, its well-being is the great object of his adminiftration. If, then, GOD, in the arrangement of the various conditions and ftations of human life, has confulted the general fecurity and intereft of mankind as a collective body,—it follows, that the condition of particular perfons, as appointed by him, is that which he fees to be expedient and neceffary, in fubordination to the good of the whole,—and ought therefore to be fubmitted to without complaint.

The condition of every perfon, as allotted by Providence, is certainly what the Supreme Wifdom fees to be fit and expedient

dient for him as an individual, as well as adapted to the general fyftem. Our CREATOR has doubtlefs the beft reafons for appointing our ftate to be fuch as we find it. Be our condition what it may, as far as it is the appointment of Providence, and not the effect of our own faulty conduct, our iniquity, indolence, inattention, or imprudence,—it is fuch as we fhould defire, or fubmit to, if all things proper to be confidered could be taken into view. He who made and governs us, is the FATHER of his creatures: he conducts all events in the wifeft methods, and for the beft purpofes; and with fo particular an attention, that not a fparrow falls to the ground,—not the moft inconfiderable contingency can happen,—without the divine permiffion.

If, then, the world be under the fuperintendence of a Supreme GOVERNOR, who is all-wife to difcern what is fitteft and beft for us; and infinitely benevolent and powerful, to determine and execute according to that difcernment;—we may conclude, that all events that happen

to

to us, and are not the refult of our own criminal or imprudent conduct, are meant for our advantage, as they are the undoubted appointments of unbounded goodnefs and unerring wifdom. All his difpenfations, however fevere or partial in their prefent appearance, are, we may be affured, wife, and merciful, and good; and that it is our duty here, and will be our happinefs here or hereafter, to acquiefce in his appointments, and pay him the homage of a willing fubmiffion.

The world was by fome of the ancients, with propriety enough, compared to a theatre, on which mankind appear, and act different parts; but thofe not fortuitoufly caft, but affigned by the DIRECTOR of the univerfe, who beft knows the characters in which it is proper for us to appear. Our duty is, to acquiefce in what is allotted us; and our fole concern ought to be, to acquit ourfelves well in our refpective parts, and fuftain well our character whilft we are upon this ftage of life. To behave otherwife, and be diffatisfied with

with our lot, is to reproach the Wisdom that presides over the theatre of nature; it is to forget that we are but of yesterday, and know nothing; that GOD is infinite in knowledge and wisdom; that the plans of his providence are far, far too extended and intricate for our limited powers to comprehend; and that, as the heavens are higher than the earth, so are his thoughts higher than our thoughts, and his ways than our ways.

Let it be considered, that to GOD we are under numberless obligations, which we can never discharge; that to him we are indebted for our being, and all the blessings consequent upon it, for which we can pay him no equivalent; that he is ever conferring favours and mercies, whilst we are incapable of making any the smallest return; that he is good to all, kinder to the worst than the best of us deserve; that therefore, though his gifts be, for wise and good reasons, distributed in unequal portions, yet none ought, nor can with justice, object to the DONOR; since,

be

be it more or less that is bestowed, it is all voluntary, unmerited favour.

Every one, therefore, ought to be satisfied with his portion; and instead of repining at the more liberal allotments of others, should be grateful for his own. Shall we complain of that BEING to whom we owe all that we enjoy, merely because he has not increased our store, when, without injustice, he might have withheld even what he has given? Does it become us, his dependents, who subsist upon his alms, and possess nothing but by favour, to prescribe the station or portion to be allotted us? No man can justly say to his MAKER, Why hast thou made me thus? Why is my rank so mean, my talents so few, my station so inferior? Why, at this feast of nature, to which I am introduced, must I sit down and take a lower place, whilst many others are bid to go up higher? For such expostulations there can be no grounds; since, for all that we have, and all we are, we are indebted to the munificence of our MAKER; whose undoubted prerogative it is, to assign to every creature in the universe his rank and station.

The almost infinite diversity of situations and conditions in which GOD has arranged mankind, is to be resolved only into his own sovereign wisdom, who may mete out his gratuitous bounty in what various measures he thinks fit. To his goodness we are indebted for our being, and for the station in being which we hold. But as it is no injury to man, that he was formed a little lower than the angels; no injury to the brute creation, that they are denied the privilege of intellectual powers; —so neither is injustice done to one man, that he is made to differ from another. Abundant reason, indeed, we have to pour out our daily gratitude to the AUTHOR of our being, for the various blessings with which he has favoured us; but no just cause to be discontented for want of what his wisdom has thought fit to withhold: *Friend, I do thee no wrong*, may our CREATOR say; *is it not lawful for me to do what I will with mine own? is thine eye evil because I am good?*

We

We may observe, that the occasions of discontent are often comparative only. We measure our wants, not by our own necessities, but by the abundance which our neighbour possesses; and are unhappy, not so much from the lowness of our own situation, as from the elevation of others. But although the conditions of mankind may be very various and unequal, yet not so is their happiness. The difference may be great in pomp, and show, and opinion; but in true enjoyment they may be nearly equal. Many there are, without any considerable advantages of fortune, easy and contented; many, who possess them all, discontented and unhappy. They who gather much of the materials of enjoyment, have nothing over; many who gather little, seem to have no lack. There is great reason to believe, that the real happiness, though not the apparent prosperity, of life, is distributed among the sons of men with a more equitable hand, and in more equal portions, than negligent observers may imagine. For happiness is something internal; it resides only in the mind; and if we search for it elsewhere, we shall never find it.

Lastly, If the causes of discontent should be, not comparative only, or imaginary, but real afflictions; if even food and raiment should be of difficult acquisition,—we may find some consolation in reflecting, that this vale of life is but short; that beyond it there lie regions of bliss, where the divine goodness will confer abundant rewards upon patience and resignation, and there amply compensate the evils we have sustained. Life is a vapour, that appeareth for a little time, and then vanisheth away, and with it all our sorrows and complaints for ever. We ought on no occasion, therefore, to repine at the appointments of Providence: for if we mourn now, we shall be comforted hereafter; if we here labour and are heavy laden, there we are sure to find rest; if heaviness should endure for the night of this life, joy cometh in the morning of the next.

Since, then, from what has been observ-ved, it may appear, that the AUTHOR of our being affigns to his creatures fuch powers, fuch a ftation or condition, as his wifdom fees to be accommodated to the general fyftem, as well as to individuals; fince GOD may, without impeachment of his goodnefs or juftice, diftribute his gifts in various portions, and we all enjoy more than we can claim or deferve; fince, tho' the allotments of mankind are very different, yet the meafure of their happinefs may be nearly equal; fince the occafions of difcontent are often comparative only, or imaginary, and, when real, can be but of fhort duration, and will be abundantly recompenfed hereafter;—we have juft grounds for fubmiffion and acquiefcence in all the divine difpenfations.

Has, then, the Giver of all good gifts difpenfed to any of us his talents with a fparing hand; has he allotted us a more fcanty portion, inferior abilities, or a lower ftation, than others?—inftead of perpetual, unavailing, and unjuftifiable diffatisfaction, let us apply with diligence to the improve-

improvement of those talents, and to the duties of that station. It is not so consequential to our happiness, what our station, what our condition is, as how we conduct ourselves in it. The favour and approbation of our LORD depend not upon the number of talents which we his stewards have received, but upon our application and management of them. Let us, then, leave it to him to appoint the talents we are to manage; let him dispense his blessings, who alone knows what will prove a blessing to us; let him assign the post we are to act in; let us be solicitous only to approve ourselves to him in the duties of it. For, be our trust great or small, our fidelity in discharging it will meet with a suitable approbation, in that state where the least will be adorned with a glory greater far than the best can deserve, or the highest of us can comprehend.

Let us then recommend ourselves to the favour of GOD, by a submissive acquiescence

quiescence in all his dispensations. Let us, with grateful complacency, accept what he bestows; and submit, with pious resignation, to what he inflicts. And as we are very insufficient judges of the means of our happiness,—ignorant of what may hurt or profit us in the final event of things, and know not what to ask or what to pray for as we ought;—let us address that all-gracious BEING, who is the dispenser of every thing that is good in itself, the sole, unerring discerner of what is good for us, and beseech him to give us those things that are good, though we ask them not; to refuse every thing that is hurtful, though we should ask it; and to impress on our hearts such an unreluctant submission to his wisdom, and so unreserved a confidence in his goodness, as may ever incline us to acquiesce, with pious complacency, in his providential appointments, and to believe that to be best for us which heaven is pleased to allot.

SERMON XXI,

Duty of Exemplary Manners.

1 THESS. v. 22.

Abstain from all appearance of evil.

THOUGH the Christian institution is much more careful to provide for integrity of heart and purity of intention, than for exterior behaviour and mere appearances; though we are every where in Scripture taught, rather to approve ourselves to GOD and our own conscience, than to be anxious how we may stand in the opinion of the world;—yet, that principal end once secured, a regard to our outward deportment is next required, not only

only as a matter of decency and prudence, but of indispensable duty.

We must be exemplary in our manners; and religiously abstain, not only from the commission, but even from the appearances of guilt. We must consider not only the rectitude of our actions in our own sight, or in the eye of heaven; but we must reflect also in what light they may appear to the world. We must not only observe strict virtue ourselves; but endeavour to let that virtue be as influential as may be on the manners of others, and become, what our SAVIOUR called his apostles, *the lights of the world;* and, in our respective spheres and stations, to let the lustre and beauty of holiness shine forth in our deportment. We ought not to hide our virtue in obscurity, nor be content with a retired unobserved piety, nor confine and immerse our religion within the closet; but we should make it the companion of our conversation, as well as of our retirements,—and by our example endeavour to

befriend

befriend and support its cause, and preserve its due reputation and esteem.

Our conduct should not only be just, but appear laudable; such as may both obtain the divine, and merit human approbation. But be it observed, we are not to make the desire of human approbation the leading motive or principle of our actions: for if human applause be indeed our only or ultimate aim, it will also be our chief or sole reward. Our SAVIOUR expressed uncommon severity against those hypocrites who, when they gave alms, would sound a trumpet to give public notice, and to assemble a concourse of people to be witnesses of their donations; when they prayed, purposely selected such places for their acts of devotion as were most in view; and, when they fasted, took care, by being of a sad countenance, to acquaint the world with their acts of penitence and austerity. These duties they performed from motives of vanity and ostentation, which ought to have proceeded from a superior and better principle

ciple of piety. It was this oftentation only that our SAVIOUR reproved; for he requires us to let our light fhine before men, and enjoins an exemplary deportment. Some motives to which I fhall proceed to offer.

1*ſt*, **Every man, from the** regard due to his own reputation and character, ought to be exemplary in his behaviour; becaufe, as the world can view only the **exterior** or furface of our actions, without being able to penetrate into their internal principles and fecret fprings,—they can form no other judgment of the intentions of the heart than what outward appearances fuggeft. The mere appearance, therefore, of evil, may be conftrued into criminality, and give the fame wound to the character as real guilt. The only queftion here is, Whether a wife and good man, whofe proper bufinefs it is to approve his conduct to GOD and his own confcience, ought to fet fuch a value upon reputation, or the opinion of the world, as to fuffer a regard for it to influence and
determine

determine his actions: especially as reputation has been often reprefented by moralifts as a delufive, precarious, and vifionary good; obtained often without merit, and loft without caufe; purchafed without defert, and beftowed without judgment?

But if we confider, that this defire of a good name was planted in the mind by the all-wife AUTHOR of our being, and that a tender concern for it is made neceffary by the original principles of our nature,—we muft prefume, that it was not planted there in vain; we muft conclude, that this under-motive of action fhould indeed be governed and regulated by a fuperior principle, but not be fuppreffed or extinguifhed. The efteem of the wife and good is the moft laudable and generous of all temporal incitements to a right behaviour; and an infenfibility to fuch efteem will be apt to terminate in an indifference to fuch actions as deferve it. *A good name*, fays Solomon, *is rather to be chofen than great riches.* Both human and divine laws have
ever

ever set a high price upon it: and all those precepts of religion which forbid calumny, defamation, and slander, presuppose them to be evils; and that a good name has a real, and not merely an imaginary, value. In many cases, so much reputation is so much power: not only reasons of prudence, therefore, but even duty, will require every man to guard his reputation, as he would preserve his influence and usefulness in the world.

One case, indeed, there is, wherein we are to pay no regard to the opinion or esteem of the world; and that is, where our adherence to duty and integrity lays us open to detraction and reproach. We are religiously to obey the dictates of duty, though the consequences be censure, calumny, or contempt. For duty is too valuable a sacrifice to be made to popular favour; and unmerited censure, a burden much lighter than guilt. For what are the mistaken reproaches of an ill-judging multitude, to the severe reproofs of an awakened conscience? or what the ill-grounded,

grounded, short-lived disesteem of men, to the just and perpetual displeasure of an offended GOD? Supported by conscious integrity, a man may well bear up under undeserved censure: but, on the other hand, if he is guilty and self-convicted, no unmerited applause can acquit him to himself; and all his popular reputation will, even in his own eye, lose its lustre and value.

But although we are not to court the approbation of the world by mean condescensions, or criminal compliances; yet the admonition in the text implies that we should, by a circumspect and prudential conduct, let our virtues appear in their true light; and not in the likeness, or with the features, of any resembling vice; that our piety may not be mistaken for hypocrisy, our charity for ostentation, humility for meanness, and the like.

Such, indeed, it must be acknowledged, is the infirmity and iniquity of mankind; their judgments are so often formed upon imperfect grounds; their opinions so often dictated

dictated by their paffions; fo ready are they to build their own reputation upon the ruins of their neighbour's; fo defirous to beftow indirect praife upon themfelves, by detecting faults, indifcretions, or foibles, in others; fo confcious of defects, and fo willing, therefore, to reduce every one to their own level;—that the moft guarded virtue cannot always avoid being mifapprehended by the inadvertent, or mifreprefented by the malevolent and envious. But though we cannot always avoid cenfure, we muft do all we can, as the apoftle inftructs us, to cut off all occafion of cenfure; though it is not in our power to infure approbation, it ought to be our endeavour to deferve it.

But, 2*dly*, Not only our own reputation, but the regard alfo that we ought to have for the glory of GOD, and the happinefs of our fellow-creatures, demands our compliance with the duty in the text. The glory of GOD is always to be confidered as terminating in the happinefs of his creatures, and not in any perfonal acquifition to HIMSELF. To promote his glory, i to promote thofe juft fentiments with regard to him, that reverence for his authority, and that due efteem of his nature and perfections, which may engage mankind to revere and obey his laws, and, by fuch obedience, to acquire an equitable claim to an heavenly inheritance. His glory, therefore, will be beft promoted by an open, apparent, and exemplary obedience to his will.

Our retired acts of piety and virtue are indeed expreffive of our perfonal reverence and fubmiffion to the DEITY, and as fuch will be approved and accepted by HIM who feeth in fecret. But he requires alfo, that we would honour him before men; and that our behaviour fhould manifeft to the world fuch an awful fenfe of his being, providence, and perfections, as may incite others to honour him by the fame virtuous conduct, and may thus render us the happy inftruments of their future felicity. We ought not to be fo contracted within ourfelves, as to centre all our

care

care and concern in our own perfonal happinefs. To fit down fatisfied with the perfuafion of having difcharged our own duty; to acquiefce in our own righteoufnefs, without regarding whether, or how much, virtue or vice, religion or wickednefs, prevail in the world,—is acting upon a narrow and imperfect principle. Imperfect, indeed, muft be that virtue which feels no concern for the honour of religion, and the future felicity of mankind; narrow muft be that man's heart which his *own* intereft, temporal or eternal, can fill. We ought, by an open and vifible attachment to duty, to exprefs our regard for the honour of GOD, and our inclination to add to the virtue and to the happinefs of the world.

A good example is a conftant admonition to goodnefs. It has a fecret influence on the manners of thofe who obferve it: it carries in it both inftruction and encouragement; equally directs and exhorts to duty: it admonifhes and corrects without offence; and has in it all the utility, without the disgustfulness of reproof. To see others, those particularly whom the world esteems, going before us in the paths of goodness, will naturally invite us to pursue their steps, and imitate their virtue. They whose eminence and distinction stamp some kind of credit on their actions, and establish in some degree the fashion in principles and manners, ought to be particularly attentive to lend their example to the support of religion and virtue. For they are as a city set on an hill; the eminence of their station sets them up to view; their manners are conspicuous, and will be observed and copied: whereas virtue in the low vale of life, is, by its situation, scarce visible, or can appear only in a very limited circle.

It ought also to be considered, that the vices of others are imputable to us when occasioned by our example. Where our conduct is criminal, its influence on others will be charged to our account, and will render us partakers and accomplices in their crimes. How far the contagion of our

our manners extends; to what vices, or to what degrees of vice, our example may have seduced or encouraged others,—is more, indeed, than we can say; but not more than we must account for. For though the influence of our vices upon the minds of others may not lie open to human observation, yet the SEARCHER of hearts sees distinctly the degrees of infection communicated by an evil example, and will adjust our punishment to the measure of our guilt.

Be it then our study, to be exemplary in our manners and deportment; since our own reputation, the glory of GOD, and the happiness of others, as well as our own, may in some measure be affected by our behaviour.

Let us not add the weight of our influence to the scale of vice; let none have it in their power to plead our example in favour of their guilt: let, rather, the purity and sanctity of our manners be a gentle reproof to the profligate and profane; let our exemplary, and, as far as in us lies, irreproachable conduct, be a silent, but continued exhortation to goodnefs; let it be our uniform, unvaried aim, to retrieve the honour of religion, to give reputation to piety, and to excel in every grace and virtue that can adorn the moral, or complete the Chriftian character; let religion be not only efteemed in fecret, but let us pay it public honour: let us not, like the Jewifh difciple, repair to our Lord in private only, and by night; but let our life and manners publifh and proclaim our attachment and obedience to him.

Let us not only avoid whatever would be criminal in ourfelves, but endeavour, by an exemplary conduct, to reform it in others. For let us remember, that he whofe good example has made one convert to religion, by extirpating a vice, or planting a virtue in the mind of another, has faved a foul alive, and provided for the everlafting felicity of an immortal being. And they whofe examples have fhone forth, and turned many to righteoufnefs, will themfelves be at laft rewarded with a fuperior meafure of glory, and fhine as the ftars for ever and ever.

SERMON XXII.

Peace of Mind the Attendant on Virtue.

PSAL. xxxvii. 38.

Keep innocency, and take heed unto the thing that is right; for that shall bring a man peace at the last.

RELIGION, though it enjoins univerfal purity,—an uniform obedience to its laws,—and grants no licence to fin; does not yet require a total exemption from all fuch failings as ftrict juftice might pronounce faulty;—does not expect in us such perfection as never to suffer ourselves to be surprised into actions which, upon a review, may appear censurable. For if this were the duty, these the terms prescribed by religion, who could comply, or live up, to such unsinning purity? There is not a just man that liveth upon the earth and sinneth not. GOD alone is absolute, immutable holiness. He is indeed pure, unclouded light; and in HIM is no darkness at all; no shades or spots in HIS nature. But the brightest human virtue is shaded with imperfections, and blotted with various defects. Our Supreme LAWGIVER, therefore, does not expect absolute perfection; but accepts us upon the much lower condition of sincerity, *i. e.* of a predominant purpose and inclination to obey him appearing in the habitual virtues of a good life. This is all the obedience that human frailty can pay, and all that the divine mercy exacts. This it is to keep innocence, and take heed to the thing that is right; and that this will bring peace to the mind, both in this life

life and the next, is a doctrine which this discourse is meant to illustrate.

Internal peace is the natural consequence, the genuine produce, of innocence and an attention to what is right. For such is the moral constitution and frame of our nature, that we cannot withhold our approbation when our conduct appears right and conformable to the laws of our MAKER. The mind can never disapprove a good action, as such; though it may indeed disapprove the defects in our good actions, and those spots and blemishes that are too visible in human characters for conscience to overlook. Though sensible of human frailty, and of the stains that are to be found in the purest virtue, it never refuses its congratulations to worthy deeds, to honest and benevolent dispositions. Have we performed a good action? have we done justly, or shown mercy? we need not search for laboured arguments to justify us to ourselves; for peace and complacency spontaneously spring up from it. Let us but take care

to

to act in compliance with the monitions of confcience; and it will diffufe a ferenity over the mind, which nothing elfe can give, and no external accidents can take away. Then, whatever ftorms may arife from without, even in the fevereft feafons of adverfity, we fhall find a calm within; we fhall find a fenfe of fecurity and confidence in our own breaft.

The happinefs, indeed, of men,—of intellectual beings, who have reflection and confcience,—muft confift in conducting themfelves fo, that Reflection and Confcience, thofe beft of friends, but moft implacable of enemies, may not be armed againft them. It is not power, wealth, reputation, honour,—it is not any thing external,—that can give reft, and eftablifh peace in the foul. As long as we are reafonable creatures, Reafon, whether we will or not, will be chiefly inftrumental in our ill or well being. Do we act reafonably and virtuoufly? Reafon or Confcience will be our bofom-friend, and we may be happy. If we act unreafonably or or criminally, Conscience, which can never be reconciled to crimes, will be our internal enemy, and we must be wretched.

And indeed nothing can make us so absolutely wretched, or give us such a total disrelish of our being, as that self-reproach which is the consequence of conscious guilt. This will indeed penetrate the soul, and wound the spirit, and fill the mind with anguish, and the countenance with confusion. It had this effect upon Cain, after shedding his brother's blood: *And the Lord said unto Cain, Why art thou wroth? and why is thy countenance fallen?*

When a man's actions are at variance with his judgment, and he lives in contradiction not only to the laws of GOD, but to the dictates and acknowledgments of his own breast; when he is at once under the dominion of his passions, and the reproach of his reason;—how is it possible he should be satisfied with himself, or ever know the pleasure of one self-approving hour? What can be more painful

painful than to be self-accused,—to be an involuntary witness against himself, and to be convicted as a criminal by his own sentence? Far from enjoying the pleasing gratulations of a good conscience, or feeling any degree of self-complacency; disturbed imaginations, bitter reflections, and secret remorse, will prey upon his mind: *There is no peace*, saith the prophet, *to the wicked.* Guilt has no resting-place; has not where to lay its head in security; can find no sanctuary from its fears, no refuge from its own reproaches. The guilty mind is like a desolate and barren waste, overrun with noxious and baneful weeds, exhibiting a deformed and melancholy scene, without a single object to invite or entertain the eye. But, on the other hand, the religious and good man, by a constant attention to the moral culture and improvement of the soul, by planting in it all the virtues, and producing the various fruits of goodness, adorns and embellishes his mind; so that to the eye of Reflection, it presents the happiest

happiest and most delightful prospect that art or nature can furnish. When we are conscious that we do what we ought, and are what duty requires us to be, as far as human frailty will permit; when we thus find all right at home, in our own breast,—we have then the enjoyment of our being, and the mind is in a placid and healthful state. For virtue is indeed to the soul, what health is to the body; and all vices are its diseases. When Religion is the principle of our actions, and we regulate our manners, and the temper of our souls, by its prescriptions, the mind is in health and ease.

But if, rejecting its salutary admonitions, we suffer ourselves to be tainted by any vicious infection,—we create to ourselves constant occasions of pain and anguish. And nothing but the variety of objects, amusements, and pleasures, which attract attention and supply entertainment, can prevent the anguish and pain which the wicked man would feel, were he seriously to reflect on his conduct. The

serious

serious reflection upon guilt is painful; and moral evil is attended with disquieting reflections, just as natural evil is with uneasy sensations.

The AUTHOR of our nature has appointed painful impressions to be made on the mind or the body, whenever we do what is injurious to the health of the one, or to the virtue of the other. And as evil actions torture the mind with its own reflections; so good actions impart agreeable perceptions to the soul, and every recollection of them repeats the pleasure. And what consideration can more effectually invite and animate us to duty, than to reflect, that the sense and memory of it will always bring pleasure to the mind? so that, with whatever reluctance we enter upon the practice of virtue, we are sure of peace and complacency, sure of no occasion of inquietude in looking back upon it. For does the consciousness of having been honest, faithful, benevolent, or charitable, ever excite in us any sorrowful sentiments of repentance? Did ever the recollection of our virtue fix a painful
sting

sting in the mind? Who ever felt any secret remorse for having done justly, **loved mercy,** or walked humbly with his GOD?

Perform your **duty faithfully to your** CREATOR and **your** fellow-creatures, and the memory of it will be **always** pleasing; —will supply an entertainment that **never** satiates. Is there trouble **in any good** action we do? the trouble is **soon** over, but the pleasure of it **is a** perpetual feast. **Do** we find pleasure in a criminal action? it is transient and short-lived; but the anguish which succeeds is a worm that never dies. It is an uncontested truth, that the practice of virtue is the practice recommended and approved by our reason,—**by that principle** which was given us **by our** CREATOR to superintend and regulate **our conduct.** To Virtue **we are** constantly **directed by** serious consideration; are attended in it with the secret approbation of **our own mind;** and after it, **entertained with the pleasures** of reflection. On the contrary, **to Vice** we are never prompted by serious consideration; never, never led by the **counsels** of reason and judgment; but are accompanied

panied in it by frequent accufations of our own heart, and purfued after it by the reproaches of a wounded confcience.

True it is, in the prefent ftate of our being, the joy of a felf-gratulating, and the torture of a felf-reproaching mind, are in a great meafure diverted and abated by various caufes; by the numerous cares, avocations, employments and amufements of life. But when life comes to a conclufion, and thofe avocations and amufements are no more; when Death clofes the fcene, and diffolves the union of body and mind, —the mind will probably be more alive to every impreffion, and its fenfibility become much more exquifite and perfect, when it is no longer clogged and incumbered with the body, and the joys and forrows of confcience may be felt in a much higher degree than we are now able to conceive. But even now experience convinces fome, a careful attention might convince all,—that the one is the higheft happinefs, the other the fevereft mifery, of our nature; that no affliction can be fo ill fupported as the anguifh of a guilty mind,

no

no pleasure equal to that of innocence and a good conscience.

But further: The internal peace which the good man enjoys, receives a great addition from this consideration, that his innocence must bring him peace at the last; that his integrity cannot fail to procure him, what nothing else can procure, the approbation and favour of that Supreme BEING, who loveth righteousness, and whose countenance will behold the upright. The opposition is not greater between light and darkness, than between virtue and vice. The one is in its nature right, good, and amiable; the other, of essential malignity, the object of detestation. Resentment and indignation are the just wages of iniquity; approbation and favour are naturally due to virtue.

And certain it is, that the infinitely righteous GOVERNOR of the world, the JUDGE of all the earth, will do right, and act in conformity to those distinctions that have an immoveable foundation in nature. Certain it is, that he will express his approbation of the one by proper rewards, and his displeasure at the other by just punishments. For what is this, but acting according to reason and rectitude? and what may, consequently, be expected from HIM who is Infinite Reason; whose countenance cannot behold iniquity without indignation, nor the upright without favour? It is his irreversible decree, a decree as immutable as the nature of good and evil, as immutable as his own nature and perfections,—that sinners shall receive the just wages of sin, and good men the reward of their labours, if not in this life, most certainly in another.

The scene of retribution, indeed, is not laid in this world; though even here virtue does not always languish unobserved and neglected. An invisible Providence often attends the steps of the righteous, and conducts them in the paths of prosperity and success. But though the practice of virtue is often profitable, always satisfactory, in this life; though it bring along with it various present blessings and rewards;—yet it insures to us infinitely more and greater in reversion.

Virtue

Virtue can look forward to futurity with confidence, and has the highest pleasure in hoping and believing, that as certainly as there is an infinitely good BEING, who governs the world; as certainly as he formed us capable of discerning the distinctions of good and evil; as certainly as he made us intellectual and accountable beings; and as certainly as there is a future state to succeed this short, transitory scene:—so certainly will the favour of GOD, and all the proper expressions of it, be hereafter the reward of the virtuous and the good. And from the firm hope and expectation of this future reward, this happiness in reversion, it is, that religious minds derive their principal enjoyment. This is their hope, their refuge, their consolation and support, that heightens and improves every pleasure, and softens and alleviates every misfortune.

If religion opened to our view no prospect of immortality, made no provision for us hereafter, and took no care of us beyond the grave; though its duties would be still in their nature right, and good, and amiable, preferable far to vice and guilt; yet it would undoubtedly come less recommended, and have an inferior claim to our regard. But since we are assured of another life to succeed the present, and of an exceeding and eternal weight of glory in it, promised to our obedience,—what does reason tell us ought to be the first object of our care? What is the one thing needful, but to secure, by our obedience, a claim to this heavenly inheritance? Virtue comes not only attended with tranquillity of mind, which is the principal satisfaction of life; with the favour of God, which is better than life; but also insures to us eternal life and felicity hereafter. It brings with it comfortable reflections, and sets before us the most agreeable prospects. It is pleasing in the act, delightful in recollection, happy in its expectations. Keep innocency, then, and take heed to the thing that is right; for that, and that alone, can bring us peace, both now and at the last.

SERMON XXIII.

Methods by which GOD has revealed his Will to Mankind.

1 TIM. ii. 4.

―― *Who will have all men to be saved, and to come unto the knowledge of the truth.*

IF we have upon our mind a serious conviction of the existence of a GOD, the Author and Governor of universal nature; and if we believe, that, this life ended, we shall enter into a more important state of being, wherein divine justice will allot rewards, or inflictions, suited to our behaviour here on earth;—we cannot but find ourselves infinitely concerned to obtain the approbation of the Supreme AR-

BITER of our fate; and, consequently, to apply our whole care and attention to discover what is his will, what conduct will recommend to his favour, and what will render us objects of his displeasure.

And in this respect we are not left to wander in darkness and uncertainty. As GOD has a sovereign claim to the obedience of his creatures, so has he sufficiently instructed us in the nature of the obedience he expects; for, as the Apostle expresses it in the text, he would have all men to be saved, and to come to the knowledge of the truth.

Let us therefore inquire, by what methods GOD has communicated to mankind the knowledge of his will, and of the duties he requires from them.

The ALMIGHTY does not indeed appear in a visible form and majesty to his creatures, to announce to them their various duties; nor does he communicate his instructions by an audible and awful voice from heaven: but the same information, the same instructions, are delivered in a way

way and manner that do not interfere with moral liberty. He speaks to us in the language of nature; he reveals his will in the still voice of reason; in the dictates of conscience, by which we are taught good and evil, and have as evident a perception of the distinction between virtue and vice, between duty and transgression, as the eye has of the beauty or deformity of objects of sight, or of the difference between light and darkness. When we are by nature taught the difference of good and evil, and our various moral duties,—who is it but the AUTHOR of nature that teaches and instructs us? If he has so framed the mind, that some actions, by his appointment, necessarily appear to us right and amiable, and worthy of reward; others wrong, and hateful, and deserving of punishment;—this is equivalent to a declaration of HIM who made us, that we ought to pursue the one, and avoid the other: that he approves, and will reward, the former; and disapproves, and will punish, the latter. If we are by nature

X 4   uniformly

uniformly led to annex the ideas of propriety, fitness, and rectitude, to certain actions,—it is a clear intimation from the AUTHOR of our being, that such actions have his approbation.

The Divine Goodness has thus made his laws sufficiently clear to all who are bound to obey them: and the promulgation of his laws, we may observe, is the completest that can be wished or imagined. For it is not made, like that of human laws, once perhaps in a solemn manner, at some public place, on some particular occasion: but it is made and repeated, constantly and perpetually, by the voice of nature, which every one must hear; and inscribed on every man's heart, in characters which he cannot but understand. Of this law we may justly indeed say, that *it is not hidden from us, neither is it far off: it is not in heaven, that we should say, Who shall go up for us to heaven, and bring it unto us? but it is very nigh unto us, in our mouth, and in our heart, that we may do it.*

The moral principle in us, whether we call it conscience, reason, or moral sense; whether we consider it as a perception of the understanding, or a sentiment of the heart, or, what seems nearest the truth, as including both;—this moral faculty points out, in most cases, the rightness or iniquity of actions, in so conspicuous and clear a light, that the most ignorant perceive it, without any previous application or instruction: and generally apprehend what is right or wrong, moral or immoral, in common behaviour, as clearly and distinctly as they perceive the difference between truth and falsehood in the most obvious propositions. Nature, that gave us corporeal organs to distinguish light and darkness, gave us also an intellectual eye, a moral power, to discern, with equal readiness and facility, right and wrong, good and evil.

This directing principle in us could be given with no other intention, than to serve as a lantern unto our feet, and a light unto our paths; to show us what course of action

action we ought to pursue, and what errors we should avoid. And as the law in our hearts was inscribed there by the hand of our CREATOR; so, in order to make it still more evidently appear that he expects and requires our obedience to this law, he has enforced it by natural sanctions, by internal rewards or punishments which are naturally consequent on the observance or violation of it. For he has so framed and constituted the human mind, that whenever we reflect upon our moral behaviour, such reflection is necessarily accompanied with a pleasing or a painful consciousness. He has annexed an inseparable sense of security and good desert to good actions, and of ill desert and danger to bad ones. An odious perception of guilt, self-reproach, and secret apprehensions of the divine displeasure, are the internal consequences of sin; and serenity, gladness of heart, self-enjoyment, and a confidence in the divine favour, are the sure attendants on virtue, and are thus the natural sanctions of the law of our nature;—clear indications

tions of the divine approbation of virtue, and difapprobation of vice; and amount to a declaration, that it is the will of the Author of our being, that we fhould purfue the former, and avoid the latter. The book of nature, then,—that book which lies open to all the world, is publifhed in all nations, written in all languages, intelligible to all people;—that is our firft revelation, and in the volume of that book we may plainly read the will of God.

But, 2*dly*, Though this book of nature, this volume of the law of reafon, in many nations, and for many ages, fupplied the place of other laws; yet God did not leave all mankind to the fuggeftions of nature or reafon alone, but, from the beginning, communicated occafional revelations to fome felect perfons in the firft ages of the world, when reafon may be fuppofed to have been lefs cultivated and improved, and confequently to have ftood in greater need of revealed inftructions. He gave afterwards a law to the people of Ifrael, and out of heaven made them to hear his voice,

voice, that he might inftruct them. This law was not indeed, like the law of reafon, univerfal and obligatory to all mankind; but was in its nature and defign a municipal law and conftitution, for the governing of one particular nation and people, who were, by civil and religious inftitutions, feparated from all people upon the face of the earth, and in a great meafure excluded from the commerce and converfation of other nations. Part of their law was adapted to their genius and prejudices; and particularly to their inclination for a pompous, exterior worfhip. God afterwards fent a fucceffion of infpired prophets, to reprove and correct the degeneracy of his people, to preferve the purity of religion, and efpecially to teach and inculcate the fuperior excellence and importance of moral virtue, then fupplanted by external obfervances.

The intention of our all-gracious CREATOR in thus revealing himfelf at fundry times to his creatures, was, doubtlefs, that they might know and obey him, and
be

be made happy by such knowledge and obedience. And still further to effectuate this merciful intention, he sent the Saviour of the world, with the last, the most authoritative and perfect revelation of his will; not to one nation or people only, like the Mosaic law,—but to all people, nations, and languages. God has indeed given his statutes and ordinances unto Israel; but he had not dealt so with any other nation, nor had the Heathen knowledge of his revealed will. But our Saviour Christ came, not only to fulfil the Jewish law, but also to be a light to lighten the Gentiles.

The law of nature which was originally, indeed, inscribed upon the heart of man, but was become much-corrupted and defaced, and almost obliterated, by error and superstition, our blessed Saviour, by his advent into the world, republished, restored to its genuine purity, confirmed with new authority, illustrated with new light, and enforced with new sanctions. He taught the purest morality in all its juft extent; gave us a complete and perfect law and rule of life; fixed our duty, and made it more plain and certain than either the law of nature or the Jewifh inftitution had done before. His whole fyftem was committed to writing, in a language at that time the moft univerfally underftood of any in the world; by which means this facred treafure of wifdom has been tranfmitted to us,—and mankind are thereby continually informed, reminded, and exhorted to the practice of their duty.

From what has been offered we may obferve, firft, the extenfive goodnefs and affection of the Supreme BEING to us his creatures, in the various provifions he has made to lead us to the knowledge and practice of duty, and to the enjoyment of that felicity which refults from it. Every part, indeed, of the divine conduct towards mankind, bears the moft evident fignatures of his attention to their happinefs. Thefe are vifible in the whole conftitution of Nature, and in all the difpenfations

fations of Providence, even thofe which regard only our temporal convenience and exterior condition; but the moſt valuable expreſſions of his goodneſs are thofe which relate to the future, eternal intereſts of our fouls. Such is that moral faculty which he has formed within us,—that candle of the LORD which he hath lighted up in every human mind, to fhow us the paths of virtue and happineſs; and ſuch alſo is that additional greater light afforded by Revelation.

Theſe are clear indications of his paternal regard and affection to men, his creatures and children; and muſt wipe off that injurious imputation which fome would fix upon him, who think, that he predeſtinated a great part of mankind to inevitable mifery; and therefore excluded them from all light of information, and fhut them up in a ſtate of unavoidable darkneſs and ignorance. Highly injurious is this opinion to the honour of HIM whofe mercies are over all his works, who would have all men to be faved, and

whofe

whose especial care it doubtless is to conduct the moral and intellectual part of his creation to that state of perfection and felicity for which he designed and framed them. He is the Saviour of all men, even of those to whom he has not communicated his inspired instructions; as he has lighted up so much knowledge in their minds, and given them so many natural notices of their duty, as, if properly attended to, would lead them to the end of religion; and did in fact enable some of the Heathen world to make a considerable progress in moral goodness, which GOD will undoubtedly acknowledge with suitable distinctions of glory.

Lastly, If GOD has assisted Christians particularly with such various means of religious instruction, and has revealed to us the knowledge of his will, both by the light of nature and of the gospel; it highly concerns us seriously to reflect upon our obligations to conform to his will, and to live up to that knowledge of it
which

which he has vouchsafed to communicate to us.

God has entirely deprived our sins of the plea of ignorance; for under the light of Revelation, added to that of Nature, ignorance cannot but be voluntary, and must itself be a crime which can admit of no extenuation. Let us consider, that all the advantages and opportunities of instruction we enjoy, are talents entrusted to our care, for the use and application of which we stand accountable: that Christians ought to go beyond the rest of the world, in piety and virtue, in proportion to those advantages: that every degree of knowledge we possess, will be an aggravation of the sins committed against it, and will add to the measure of our punishment, and to the number of our stripes: that if the Heathen world, who had no other knowledge of the divine will than what they could collect from the visible works of the Creator, and from the light of unassisted Reason, were left without excuse for not obeying the direction of

that

that light; and if he also who despised the law of Moses, died without mercy,—how shall we escape, if we neglect so much greater means of salvation? For unto whomsoever much is given, of him much will be required. Better it had been for us not to have known the way of righteousness, than, after we have known it, to turn from the holy commandment delivered to us. What can excuse or extenuate the guilt of the Christian offender, who sins against light and conviction with a clear view of the rule of his duty, and with a deliberate contempt and determined neglect of it? What evasions can he find to acquit him to the world, to himself, or, what is of infinitely higher concern, to the Supreme Judge of all the earth?

Let us, then, be careful to profit by the advantages we enjoy, and not pervert the mercies of the gospel into an occasion of adding to our condemnation; let not the very means of salvation become the saddest aggravation of our ruin; let us henceforth walk

walk as children of light; and let thofe beams of divine knowledge which illuminate our minds, convey their falutary influence into our hearts, and appear confpicuous in all the virtues of a good life. Happy are we that know thefe things; much happier ftill, if we are careful to do them. Then may we look forward with humble confidence to the laft awful tribunal, in expectation of the mercy of our JUDGE;—and pioufly hope, that he who has in this world granted us the knowledge of his truth, will in the world to come give us life everlafting.

SERMON XXIV.

General instances of God's goodness to Men.

PSAL. cvii. 31.

O that men would therefore praise the Lord for his goodness, and declare the wonders that he doth for the children of men.

RELIGION, both natural and revealed, is founded upon this principle, That God, the Creator of all things, is a Being infinitely good and benevolent. On this principle, as on a firm foundation, rest all our better hopes. And as this is of all truths the most important, so to

this

this the whole creation bears ample testimony. For as the DEITY is supreme, independent, self-sufficient, incapable of having any private end to serve,—it is wholly inconceivable, **what** besides his goodness, or disposition to communicate happiness, could at first induce him to confer existence on his creatures, or what afterwards can engage him to the exertion of his power in preserving and governing them. The happiness of his creatures was questionless the object he had in view when he gave birth to the creation. It was for this the world was produced, and for this it is continued and governed. This is the **end,** the sole end conceivable by us, of the creation and providence.

As the goodness of the DEITY must ever be a pleasing object of contemplation, and nothing can be a better ground of consolation and joy to his creatures,—I shall in this discourse select and point out some evident and general instances of his goodness; some of the wonders that he doeth for the children of men.

I. The

I. The goodness of the Supreme Being is apparent in the regular and liberal provision he makes for the sustenance and support of the numerous tribes of his creatures, and in the annual distributions of his bounty to them. What almost infinite multitudes of various beings are his dependents, and subsist by the alms of his mercy! How extensive and astonishing is that providence which in one view comprehends the whole world, and the support of every creature in it, and produces stores adequate to such an immense and continual consumption! *The eyes of all wait upon God; he openeth his hand, and filleth all things living with plenteousness.*

The human species seem to be indeed especial objects of his providential care. He is kind to us above our deserts, and beyond our hopes. All our various, still returning wants, are supplied by his bounteous hand. Which way soever we turn our eyes, we find ourselves encompassed with the mercies of God, and they surround us on every side. How amazing is his

his attention to the children of men, in giving us *rain from heaven, and fruitful seasons, filling our hearts with food and gladness!* For us *he visiteth the earth, and blesseth it. He watereth her furrows, sendeth rain into the little valleys thereof, blesseth the increase of it, and crowneth the year with his goodness.*

When our blessed SAVIOUR, with a few loaves, compassionately fed a numerous multitude; astonished at the miracle, they justly supposed him to be some great Personage invested with power from Heaven. But how much more astonishing is that kind exertion of divine goodness, which, by an annual miracle, if we may so call it, multiplies the fruits of the ground, and gives food for all the nations of the earth,—who subsist upon the regular returns of this bounty, and are fed with bread from heaven? It is only the regularity of this appearance, and its periodical return at stated seasons, that makes it cease to be miraculous; but it is in its nature as wonderful and astonishing, as that

that a few loaves should, in our SAVIOUR's hand, grow, and be multiplied to the sustenance of a great multitude. We are apt, indeed, to look upon the produce of the earth as our own, and to consider it as the debt of Nature, rather than the bounty of Providence; whereas we ought to regard it as the alms of our CREATOR, which he distributes to us his creatures, who depend on the regular supplies, the annual donations, of his charity, for our food and subsistence.

II. But our merciful GOD not only liberally provides for our sustenance, and supplies our wants, but his kind providence also protects and watches over us with a paternal affection; regards us, though we forget him; is mindful of us, when we are neglectful of ourselves; renews his mercy to us every morning; is patient, though we provoke him every day. No moment of our lives is destitute of his care; no accident can find us unguarded by his watchful eye. His powerful, though unseen arm, defends us, as with a shield,

from

from many known, many unknown evils. Seldom a day paſſes, at the cloſe of which we have not reaſon to thank God for it. From the moment of our birth to the preſent hour, he has ſupported and bleſſed us with a thouſand mercies. When we conſider our preſervation amidſt all the hazards and dangers, the inward diſeaſes, the outward violences, our frail nature is liable to; when we reflect upon all the various evils we have eſcaped, the ſucceſſes we have obtained, and the bleſſings we have enjoyed; muſt we not feel a grateful ſenſe of the divine favour and protection? Many favourable paſſages of his providence, many inſtances of his more immediate hand, relieving our wants, aiding our infirmities, ſupporting us under troubles, extricating us from difficulties, or protecting us from dangers, we muſt indeed be inattentive if we have not obſerved, and ungrateful if we forget.

And what can we give unto the Lord, or what does he require, for all the benefits

fits that he hath done unto us? No difficult, oppressive, or severe services; nothing but the observance of such duties as their natural excellence, amiableness, and utility, must, antecedently to any divine injunction, have recommended to our attention and esteem.——Which leads,

III. To another instance of the divine goodness, viz. his adapting his laws to our nature, and requiring only those services which are the proper instruments and means of our happiness, are subservient and essential to the security and wellbeing of individuals, and to the public interest and tranquillity of the world: A conduct this, worthy of the FATHER of mankind, and clearly expressive of his paternal affection to us. GOD has an absolute, unlimited, dominion over his creatures; and if he had bid us do some great thing, we must have done it. He might, if he had so pleased, have imposed heavy burdens; might have required, under the severest penalties, the observance of injunctions to which our nature was most averse,

and

and where we muſt have obeyed with reluctance.

But the merciful AUTHOR of our being has not dealt thus ſeverely with us. In the duties he has enjoined, he has not ſo much exerciſed his ſovereignty, as he has expreſſed his goodneſs; in requiring obedience to them, he is conferring a favour. They come recommended to us by their own eſſential, intrinſic worth. Approved by the natural ſentiments of the heart, they muſt, independently of any divine authority or ſanction, always have commanded our regard. How much happineſs did the AUTHOR of our nature intend us, when he gave us theſe laws, the laws of kindneſs,—meant to eſtabliſh peace upon earth; to ſubdue all thoſe irregular, unruly paſſions, which are the ſources of private differences, or public diſcord; and to introduce into the world an inferior, temporary heaven,—a ſtate of univerſal harmony, benevolence, and happineſs? Such is the ſpirit and genius of the divine laws; evident indications of the benevolence of
their

their Author, and of his kind attention to the happiness of his creatures.

IV. But the goodness of God was most eminently displayed in the mission of his Son into the world for us, and our salvation. The temporal blessings with which his providence supplies our wants in this life, and the laws with which he has favoured us for the direction of our conduct, are indeed clear expressions of his loving-kindness, and demand every acknowledgement that gratitude can offer. But yet the condition of our present being is of small moment, in comparison of that immortal state which is to succeed it: and little it would avail us to be supplied by his bounty with the conveniences and comforts of this world, and to be instructed by his laws how to obtain all the felicity of the next, if every violation of those laws were to forfeit that felicity, and bring down upon us the inflictions of his justice; if our sins were to pursue us for ever, and no method of atonement were appointed

appointed to propitiate the DEITY, and expiate our offences.

For ever adored, then, be that infinite goodness, which inclined him to look with an eye of pity upon our offences; to plan a method by which justice and mercy might meet together; and to accept the sufferings of a REDEEMER, as a propitiatory oblation, **an expiatory** sacrifice, for the sins of his creatures. *Blessed, then, be the God and Father of our Lord Jesus Christ, who, according to his abundant mercy, hath begotten us again unto a lively hope by the death of Christ, to **an inheritance** incorruptible, reserved in heaven for us.*——Which leads me,

V. To consider **the** last most glorious display of the divine goodness, viz. that heavenly inheritance, that never-ceasing felicity, promised in the Gospel to those who obey its **laws.**

And here we **may** observe, **that** though the happiness **of his creatures** is the end which the CREATOR and SOVEREIGN of the world has in view **in** his providence

and

and government; yet he purfues this end by fuch methods only as his moral perfections require. Divine goodnefs is a difpofition, not to make all his creatures indifcriminately happy in any poffible way; but to make the juft, the good, the merciful, and upright, happy. And to thofe he has promifed fuch good things as pafs man's underftanding. We have no powers, no faculties, able to reach that fublimity of happinefs which the righteous fhall enjoy in another world.

But though the fpecific nature or the particulars of that felicity which the divine goodnefs hath prepared for us, are not, cannot, be revealed; yet thus much we know, that as far as the heavens are high above the earth, fo far will the future manfions of blefs tranfcend the moft exquifite enjoyments here below. For in heaven there will be fulnefs of joy; it will be complete and perfect, fuited to the fpiritual nature of the foul, and more than equal to its moft enlarged defires; not like earthly pleafures, promifing in expectation,

tation, and fallacious in poffeffion; not embittered with any painful mixture; not interrupted by difquieting fufpicions, nor fucceeded by uneafy terrors;—but abounding with joys unfpeakable and full of glory; a glory, in comparifon of which the brighteft fcenes of worldly pleafures are but fhadows and illufions. As the fouls of juft men are there made perfect, fo their pleafures are there pure and unmingled; worthy of unbounded goodnefs to beftow, and fit for immortal fpirits to receive.

And further: As the joys of heaven are full, complete, and fatisfactory, fo alfo are they permanent and perpetual,—subject to no abatement, interruption, or decay; not only large beyond our utmoft wifhes, but lafting as our immortal fouls. Heaven and earth may pafs away; the elements may melt with fervent heat; the earth, and the works that are therein, may be burnt up:—but our happinefs fhall continue firm and ftable, as invariable in its nature as exquifite in its glory; will
never,

never, never come to an end, nor ever approach nearer to it; but after the longeſt duration we can conceive,—after all the millions of years or ages that the power of numbers can add together,—will be but commencing, and as far as ever from a period.

How eſtimable, how infinitely eſtimable, then, is this gift of exiſtence, which is never to be reſumed! How ſupremely adorable the goodneſs which confers it! What returns can we make for all the various expreſſions of the divine favour? With what ſincerity of heart, what impreſſions of piety, what fervour of devotion, ſhould our ſouls bleſs the Lord, and all that is within us praiſe his holy name! With what ardor of affection ought we to love him, who hath ſo loved us! Let us, with the deepeſt reverence of ſoul, look up to the merciful Author of our being, and implore him to add one more to all his other bleſſings; to give us an heart duly ſenſible of them,—itſelf the greateſt we can poſſeſs.

Let

Let us often reflect, what grateful acknowledgments are due, what an immense debt we owe, and must for ever owe, to HIM whose mercies give us all we have, and will hereafter exceed all we can desire; and be it remembered, that the best method of discharging this debt, is by a regular obedience to his laws, and a constant attention to form our manners by the example of his goodness. Has the FATHER of the Universe, the PARENT of Good, supplied us with whatever is necessary to our subsistence, convenient for use, or pleasant for enjoyment? is his goodness unlimited, and his hand ever open to fill all things living with plenteousness?—let us, within our limited sphere, do good to all, and diffuse mercy over all our works; let us be merciful as HE is merciful, and render ourselves the agents of his providence, by distributing his alms, and conveying his bounty, to the indigent and needy.

Has the SOVEREIGN of the world given us laws to be a lamp unto our feet, and a light unto our paths, to guide our steps in the way of peace, and to conduct us to mansions of future felicity? let us express some little similitude of the divine conduct, by our admonitions and instructions; by our endeavours to inform the ignorant, to reclaim the vitious, and direct the weak. Is the Supreme BEING merciful and gracious; and does he forgive iniquity and transgression, and sin? let us have compassion on our fellow-servants, as our LORD hath pity upon us; let us forgive others their offences, as GOD, for CHRIST's sake, hath forgiven ours; and let us, in a word, by a pious imitation of the divine goodness during our abode on earth, endeavour to obtain an admission to that glorious display, those inconceivable manifestations of it, which he hath reserved for our reward in heaven.

SERMON XXV.

Men Sojourners upon Earth.

Preached on New-year's Day.

Heb. xiii. 14.

Here we have no continuing city, but we seek one to come.

THE text is a short, but striking description, of the state and condition of human life: intimating, that Nature has not assigned us this world for a permanent habitation; that we come not here to stay and make our abode; that we are only travellers in our way to eternity, every day setting out on our journey, hastening forwards as fast as time can carry us; and that life's short pilgrimage must be quickly at an end. So sensibly felt, and so universally acknowledged, is indeed this inevitable lot of human nature, that it should seem unnecessary to be reminded of it; it should seem, that the reflection cannot escape us, if we reflect at all. But the misfortune is, while we all own this in general, each neglects to bring home to himself the unwelcome truth; we seem to dismiss it from our thoughts, whenever it intrudes, and live as if we knew it not.

From the words of the text, therefore, I shall take occasion, 1*st*, To remind us of the short and transitory condition of human life; and, 2*dly*, Shall from thence deduce some inferences and reflections.

I. No sooner are we capable of looking round us, and considering the frame of our nature, and the condition of our being, than we may observe, that, derived from dust, we naturally hasten to dust again: that none can claim the privilege of an

exemp-

exemption from the common necessity: that man cometh up, and is cut down, like a flower: that the human, like the vegetable race, have their periods of growth and declension; and are either cut down by the hand of violence, or soon fade and drop of themselves. Strangers and sojourners here, as were all our fathers, we soon pass away, and are gone.

Nature, in her most common appearances, is ever reminding us of the transience of our state, in the succession of day and night, and the rotation of the seasons; is always admonishing us of the lapse of time, and the decay of life. The day no sooner dawns, than it begins to decline, and expires in darkness. We, in like manner, as soon as we are born, begin to draw to an end. The various seasons of the year hasten to complete their short periods. Human life has also its different seasons, which quickly finish their appointed course. A little time soon passeth away in the spring and verdure of infancy; a little more, and the bloom of youth fades, and is lost; a little more withers the strength and vigour of our riper years; and if we live still longer, to the winter of our age, a little time then lays our infirmities in the dust. And thus days and years glide on in quick and constant succession: we are borne along the silent, but rapid stream of time; and are soon conveyed down to that boundless ocean from whence none ever return.

The Scripture, in a great variety of allusions, represents the shortness of human life, and compares it to a wind that passeth away, and cometh not again; to a tale that is told, and forgotten; to a vapour, that appeareth for a little time, and vanisheth away. It admonishes us, that our days are swifter than a post; that they pass away as the swift ships, and as the eagle that hasteth to the prey; that man cometh forth like a flower, and is cut down; that he flieth also as a shadow, and continueth not.

II. I proceed to deduce some Reflections and Inferences from the short duration

and

and tranfitory condition of human life. Melancholy, indeed, would be the reflection, that we pafs away as a fhadow, and fade as the flowers of the field, and that life muft fo quickly come to an end, if this life were the whole of our exiftence, and we had no profpect and no hope beyond it. But, fetting afide other confiderations, the fhort term of our exiftence here may give us grounds to hope, that it will be renewed and prolonged hereafter. For can we think, that man was not defigned by his MAKER to attain that perfection in wifdom, and virtue, and happinefs, of which his nature is fufceptive? Can we imagine, that he is only to enter into the paths of knowledge; and, when he has made fome fhort progrefs, and is better able to proceed, that he is to proceed no farther? or, when he has begun to adorn his foul with wifdom, and ennoble it with virtue, and is moft fit to live, that he is to live no more? Can we believe, that we were introduced into this theatre of nature, only to go out again? or that at moft we are just to appear, and act a short part upon this stage, and show what farther improvements we are capable of;—and then, however well our character has been sustained, to be dismissed, and seen no more? Can this be the end of our being, this all the business of life? and is the curtain then to drop, and the scene to close for ever? Can we think that we were thus formed, like some insects, to be the creatures only, as it were, of a day; to flutter about a while, in the short sunshine of life, and then to be extinct for ever?

Creatures inferior to the human species attain here, in their present state, all the perfection their capacities can admit: their faculties shoot up to their full growth; and were they to live for ever, would for ever continue to be what they are. Whereas very different is the frame of the human mind: it is formed for a perpetual growth in wisdom, for an everlasting progress towards supreme perfection. But in this life, the wisest of men fall far short of those improvements, and that perfection,

for

for which Nature designed them: in understanding they are still children, still in a state of infancy, in comparison of that intellectual maturity to which they might arrive hereafter. Has the AUTHOR of nature, who can do nothing in vain, formed us with such extensive capacities, for so inconsiderable purposes? May we not rather be assured, from that wisdom which shines conspicuous in all his works, that man, when he dies, does not cease to be; that death translates us to another state; that this world is only a nursery for the next; that we here receive the first rudiments only of our being, to be afterwards transplanted into some happier climate, where we shall grow up to the utmost perfection of our nature, and flourish in immortal vigour to endless ages?

2*dly*, Meditation on our short and uncertain state in this world may wean us from an overfondness for any thing in it. This world is not our home; we have here no continuing city; we are only travellers in our pilgrimage through the world, and

and should not suffer our affections to be too much engaged by the conveniences or pleasures we may occasionally meet with, as we cannot stay to enjoy them long; they are not our own, and we must shortly take our leave of them. Whatever entertainment or accommodations, then, we may meet with in the several stages on our road to eternity; we ought to regard them with the indifference of a guest that tarries but a day.

Due reflection on the narrow limits of human life, may balance all the seducements we meet with in it. When we consider how soon life will come to an end; its pleasures, profits, possessions, all that the world calls happiness, must lose much of their reputed value, and sink in our estimation. For why should we set our whole affections on objects which we must one day, may to day, be obliged to relinquish and forsake? Why labour and wear out life, in the anxious, but fruitless, pursuit of what we must quit almost as soon as acquired? Why all this extreme attention to add field to field, and houfe to houfe, as if life and its enjoyments were never to have an end, fince we are here only ftrangers and fojourners, and muft foon remove our habitation; and then, whofe fhall all thefe things be?

We furely forget how fhort and fleeting life is, when we expend it wholly on temporary objects. Do we employ all our cares in accumulating and laying up much goods for many years? confider for how fhort a term we are to poffefs them. Confider that we are on the road to another world, travelling with fpeed to our eternal home, whither riches will not follow, and where they cannot profit us, unlefs we are now careful to remit them thither in acts of goodnefs, beneficence, and mercy. Let the ambitious man, who is impatient to obtain fome high ftation of dignity and honour, let him vifit (in imagination at leaft) the awful manfions of the dead; and let him reflect, that foon he alfo muft be added to the number, muft be fummoned to pay the fame debt of nature, be blended

with

with the same common earth, his honours, like theirs, laid in the dust, and a narrow grave be one day all that the most successful ambition can possess. Is pleasure our object? we are departing and flying from it, as fast as the wings of time can bear us, even at the very instant we mean to pursue it.

In a word, the short and precarious tenure we have of the riches, honours, or pleasures of life, is a consideration which, properly attended to, would naturally moderate our affection to them. Were we to reflect, how soon we must, and how suddenly we may, bid adieu to the world, we should set no high price upon it. We should rather endeavour to disengage ourselves, and become indifferent to its enjoyments, that we may, without embarrassment or discompofure, take a final leave, (for a final leave we must take); and in the mean time may employ our temporal life in the great purpose of insuring that which is eternal. And would we but attend to the information that Religion gives us us concerning the felicity of that eternal state, we should set no value on any thing here below, but as it might serve to accommodate us in our passage to a better country; we would no longer suffer our minds, like our bodies, to be confined to the earth: nothing would detain our affections here; they would rise above all temporal objects, and ascend, as we hope our souls will do, from earth to heaven, from time to eternity.

3*dly*, The consideration of the shortness of life may assist us in supporting us under its afflictions. As we are here but pilgrims and strangers, we may expect to meet with the usual inconveniences and disasters of travellers, and that evil may sometimes befal us in the way. But under such circumstances, we may always find consolation in reflecting, that our pilgrimage here cannot be of long continuance: that whatever difficulties we may encounter, whatever labours we sustain; however rigorous the seasons may be, or to whatever storms we are exposed:—yet that the vale of life is but short, that beyond it there lies a region

gion of perpetual serenity, never clouded with evil, where no storms invade, no tempests ever approach. We may always support ourselves under sufferings, as we can always see a period of them, and have a prospect of those mansions of peace whither afflictions cannot pursue us, and where it will be indifferent to us what our condition has been here.

If, indeed, we had been born never to die,—if we had been doomed to live for ever in this world,—infinite weight would have been added to our afflictions, as they might thereby have become irremediable and eternal. But, happily for us, life will come to an end, and all our sufferings will end with it. And no troubles need much to afflict us, if we consider Heaven as our home, and this life only as a passage to a better, where our light afflictions will be overpaid with an unfading crown of glory. All the difficulties and labours we now sustain, will in a short time be forgotten, and be as if they had never been. And of what mighty consequence is it if we suffer here, provided we escape the sufferings

ings hereafter; or, if we are denied our good things in this world, if we receive them with eternal intereſt in the next?

Laſtly, If the time of our ſojourning in this world be but ſhort and momentary, in compariſon of the next,—let the great and habitual object of our attention be that ſtate which may ſoon begin, but can never end. If " we have here no continuing city, let us ſeek one to come." Let us remember, that we are here travellers only; temporary, not fixed inhabitants: that our ſecond, better reſidence, is beyond the grave: that there is the country of our reſt and happinneſs, our home, and the end of our being: that to that better country we are haſtening apace, and that every revolving year brings us nearer to it.

At this ſeaſon, it muſt naturally occur, that as one year more of life is now elapſed, and we have conſequently a year leſs to live, we are a ſtep nearer to eternity, and ought therefore to be more vigilant in our preparation for it. May we all attend to this obvious, but important, yet neglected conſideration; may the preſent season be to all of us the commencement of a new and better obedience; may we all resolve, so to number our days, that we may apply our hearts unto wisdom,—that wisdom which cometh from above, and teaches us to fix our affections there; may each succeeding year (if Heaven vouchsafes us a succession of years) find us proceeding in goodness, as we advance in age,—going on still towards perfection, as we draw nearer to the period of life; may our religious progress keep pace with the fleeting years; may we seize them as they approach, and engage them in the service of wisdom and virtue!—So may we hope, when we bring our years to an end; when Nature summons us to depart hence; when we have finished our pilgrimage through this vale of life, and must no longer be permitted to sojourn here below;—so may we hope, that we may be deemed worthy of the rewards of virtue; worthy to be admitted into everlasting habitations, to the blessed mansions of immortality, to a continuing city, the city of the living God, where we shall for ever dwell.

SER-

SERMON XXVI.

Againſt Evil-ſpeaking.

JAM. iv. 11.

Speak not evil one of another.

IT is in many inſtances obſervable, that what is of the greateſt utility to mankind, may, by miſapplication, be productive of the moſt pernicious effects; and that the beſt things, by abuſe and corruption, may become the worſt. An obvious confirmation of this is the abuſe of that faculty, the intention of which we pervert when we ſpeak evil one of another. The faculty of language is a diſtinguiſhing mark of our MAKER's superior regard to mankind: and his design in conferring it was, doubtless, to elevate us above the herds of the field; to promote all the purposes of social life; to enable us to inform each other of the otherwise illegible characters of the heart; to consult together for mutual or general benefit; and to unite mankind in close society by the ties of converse and friendship.

But too often we see this power, given for the noblest and best, perverted to the worst of purposes, and employed to disturb, disorder, and embroil mankind, instead of rendering them, what Nature and Religion intended,—mutual helps and comforts. Among the various perversions of this power, there are few in their nature so infamous, none perhaps in practice so universal, as the crime of Evil-speaking. For, how ready a propension do we observe in mankind to assume a kind of jurisdiction over others; to erect, as it were, private courts of inquisition; to sit in judgement upon characters; and to pass sentence,

tence, not as truth and reason, as charity, or equity, or justice, direct,—but too often according to the evidence given by self-conceit and vanity, envy or pride, resentment or malice? For these are the false witnesses that rise up against our neighbour, and prevail with us to condemn him; these are the passions that tincture the behaviour, and give a colour to the manners of mankind, too apparent to escape the eye of the slightest observer.

The envious feel a most sensible pleasure in building their own reputation upon the ruins of another. The vain and the proud never taste a more exquisite satisfaction, than when they add a lustre to their own character, and exhibit it in the fairest light, by throwing into shade the merits of others. The malicious and resentful, delight in pulling down the highest characters, blackening the fairest, distorting the most upright, and in misrepresenting all.

But, however agreeable this vice of evil-speaking may appear to corrupt passions, it can never be reconciled to the laws of Reason, nor to the principles of Religion, both of which equally prohibit and condemn the practice of the slanderer.

I shall in this discourse consider, 1*st*, The nature and extent of this vice of evil-speaking; and, 2*dly*, Shall offer some considerations to discourage so common, but iniquitous, a practice.

I. By evil-speaking may be understood any manner of expression which tends to impair the reputation of another; to detract from the esteem he possesses; to diminish the current value that is put upon him, and for which he has been generally received; and to make him pass for less in the public estimation than before.

That it may appear when, and how far, we become guilty of this crime, it may be proper to trace it in its several kinds and degrees.—The highest and most flagitious species of this crime is, when a false testimony is deliberately given in a court of judicature, injurious to the person, property,

perty, or character, of our neighbour. This crime is so shameful a prostitution of conscience,—the guilt of it is blackened by such various aggravations; as it is injurious to the common interests of mankind; a violation of the highest and most sacred sanction that can be given to a testimony; committed, not by inadvertence or surprise, but in the most solemn and deliberate manner, with a determined contempt of laws both human and divine;— it is such a complication of iniquity and impiety, so utterly subversive of truth, justice, and equity, and of the public good and order and peace of society—that a false witness is justly beheld with detestation, as a common enemy of mankind, and his name deservedly branded with the deepest characters of infamy.

2*dly,* Another degree of evil-speaking is, when, with equal, though less avowed virulence, we blot the character, and stain the honour, of others, in common conversation, by aspersions which we know to be false and calumnious. Highly injurious,

rious is this practice, and admits of no vindication. It robs our neighbour of his property; for every one's good name is his property, to which he has an undoubted right till it be juſtly forfeited. It deprives him of a poſſeſſion which is, and muſt be, highly valued; for a tender concern for a good name is made dear to us by the original principles of our minds, and is a part of our nature. And what adds to the injury is, that it is often in a great meaſure irreparable; for the wounds given to a reputation are not only painful, but are ſeldom, and with difficulty, healed. The ſlanderer, then, who forgets or propagates known defamation, is criminal in the next degree to him who bears falſe witneſs againſt his neighbour in a court of juſtice.

3*dly*, Another more prevailing, though leſs malignant, ſpecies of this vice, is the ſpreading defamatory reports of others, without competent examination, or ſufficient knowledge of the truth of them. Under this head may be compriſed various

ous methods and arts of defamation; some more gross, avowed, and direct; others more concealed, subtle, and refined. This species of slander is capable of various degrees of aggravation. The most guilty are they, who, with malevolent intention, circulate the uncertain reports of calumny; the least criminal, though far from being innocent, is the inadvertent, undesigning slanderer,—who, without malice, or resentment or envy, for mere amusement, feasts, as it were, on the supposed foibles of other characters, and serves them up for the entertainment of his guests.

But here it may be proper to observe, that every censure of another's faults does **not come** under the character of defamation. It is allowable, *e. g.* to disclose a person's faults **to a** friend, in the sacredness of friendship, without any intention to stigmatise or injure; for this is only, what it is often said to be, " thinking aloud:"—or, to the world, when it becomes necessary to our own just self-defence; for we are nowhere required to love our neighbour better than ourselves. It is allowable also to detect a person's vices, to pull off the mask from a character, and show its true features to the innocent and unsuspecting, who we apprehend may suffer by entertaining too favourable sentiments, and reposing too entire a confidence in him: for it is often of consequence to the security of individuals, of a neighbourhood, and of a community, that the characters of the dishonest, as well as of the just and good, should be sufficiently known. We may likewise censure all open offenders. Such persons should meet with infamy, as public as their offence; for infamy is as much a due punishment for evil-doers, as praise is the just reward of them that do well. But, with these exceptions, it is a duty not to speak evil one of another, and to avoid whatever has the malignant aspect or appearance of slander.——Which brings me,

II. To offer some considerations in order to discourage this practice.

1*st*, We should be cautious and temperate

perate in the censure we pass on the conduct of others, lest we should happen to do them injustice: for we can only judge by appearances, which are often equivocal and fallacious. Actions may have the appearance of evil, which in themselves were innocent or laudable. We cannot discern the heart, or its intentions; but yet these internal springs are necessary to be known, before we can be capable of forming an accurate and equal judgment concerning the conduct of others. It is the intention that determines the moral nature of the action; but the innocence or guilt of actions may often depend on circumstances which can be known only to God and to Conscience. The human heart is so impenetrable, except to HIM that made it; and the moral nature of actions varies so much, according to the different motives which gave them birth,—that, in all cases, our judgments concerning them ought to be given with caution, and tempered with candour.

' 2*dly*, Let us reflect, how illiberal, how

malevolent, is the practice of entertaining ourselves or others, at the expence of our neighbour's good name. To see this in a true light, let us recollect, what we felt, what were our sensations, when any attempt was made upon our character, or any treacherous wound given to our reputation. Such, and so painful, we may conclude, will be the feelings of another in the same circumstances; and our conscience will tell us, that we ought not to be guilty of that behaviour to others, which we would resent when offered to ourselves. Reputation is a species of property always highly valued by its owner. It is one of the last things a liberal mind would submit to lose, and by some has been held in superior estimation to life itself. It is what a wise and good man regards as a valuable possession; and, next to a good Conscience, is the best support where other treasures are wanting. But if we rob or defraud him of this possession, this treasure, this pearl, which no price can purchase,—we may do him an injury

greater

greater than we can either estimate or repair. It may be impossible to make an estimate of the injury, as we cannot with certainty know what benefit he might have received, if no disadvantageous impression had been given of him: and it is seldom in our power to make reparation by any after-attempts to clear up his character; for **the vindication of** an injured character never extends so far or spreads so wide, is never so quickly propagated nor so well received, as the reproach.

How much more humane and generous is it, to stand up in defence of our neighbour's fame; to rescue his character when attacked; and to heal it when wounded; to do justice to his merits, and to extenuate his failings; to produce his good qualities into light, and to throw a veil over his misconduct? In some circumstances, to mention the good, or barely to conceal the evil, we know of another, may be as expressive of benevolence, and as kind an act of charity, as to relieve him in his greatest necessities. And in this particular, whatever

ever may be our station of life, we all have it in our power to be charitable. Charity, in other instances, may be an expensive, may be an inconvenient, perhaps an impracticable duty; but this alms the most indigent may bestow, and the most avaricious need not grudge: a good word is a cheap and easy donation, that costs us nothing.

3*dly*, Let us consider, how much better we should be employed, if, instead of being quick in discerning, malignant in marking, and severe in reprehending, the faults or foibles of others, we would turn our eyes inward, and be attentive to our own. Were these to be placed in a distinct view before us, the consciousness of failings would dictate to us that candour in respect to the actions of others, which we would find so necessary to a favourable construction of our own. Happy were it for mankind, if they would reflect with severity on their own misconduct, and with tenderness on that of their neighbour; if they would consider their own defects with

with the rigour of juftice, thofe of others with the foftenings of humanity; if they would be lefs watchful to fpy out the leaft mote in another's eye, whilft they are inattentive to the beam in their own. A perfect character is nowhere to be found. The moſt accompliſhed of human beings have their failings, the beſt their infirmities, the moſt prudent their indifcretions. Let us, with a careful and impartial eye, look into ourfelves, and we fhall there fee enough to make us lefs forward to cenfure and calumniate. The ſtricteſt inquirers into their own, are the moſt candid interpreters of others conduct. He who knows and has well confidered his own weaknefs, will be fevere on none but himſelf; and feverity then becomes juſt and laudable, when our own mifdeeds are the fubjects of it.

Laftly, Let it be obferved, that words are not of fo flight a value, in a moral eſtimate, as fome may apprehend. All fin iſſues from the heart; and whether it appears in language or action, the guilt may

be

be the same. *Whoso bridleth not his tongue*, the scripture informs us, *his religion is vain*. By our words, we are told, we shall be justified, and by our words condemned. And this vice of evil-speaking is always enumerated among those sins for which we must give a severe account at the day of judgment.

If, then, we desire a favourable sentence from our heavenly JUDGE, let us, even in our words and conversation, show that lenity and candour to others, which we shall all stand in need of at that great and awful day: and then we may hope, our lenity to others may plead for compassion to ourselves; and that GOD will be as merciful to our failings as we have been tender to those of our brethren. *Let all bitterness*, then, *and wrath, and anger, and clamour, and evil-speaking, be put away from you, with all malice; and be ye kind one to another, tender-hearted, forgiving one another, as God for Christ's sake forgiveth you.*

SERMON XXVII.

On Vitious Habits.

JER. xiii. 23.

Can the Ethiopian change his skin, or the leopard his spots? then may ye also do good that are accustomed to do evil.

FEW persons, perhaps, there are so totally devoid of principle, as not to believe their existence in a future state; and few so lost to all sentiments of goodness, so hardened against all impressions of duty, as not, in consequence of that belief, to form some occasional purposes of reforming their manners, and providing for

that

that exiſtence. For it is not poſſible to extinguiſh in ourſelves the deſire of happineſs; nor is it eaſy to ſuppreſs our natural perceptions of the criminality of ſin, or our fear of the inflictions conſequent upon it. The ſinner, therefore, when reproached by conſcience, acknowledges his guilt; but yet is apt to perſiſt in his vices, with a view of blotting them out by future repentance and reformation. Secure, as he thinks, in this illuſion, he poſtpones to ſome diſtant indeterminate period, the important duty; not conſidering, that by perſevering in the path of iniquity, and going on from ſin to ſin, his retreat becomes every day more difficult and impracticable, and he loſes both the inclination, and almoſt the power of reforming.

In order, then, to prevent this ſelf-deception, we may do well to conſider the words of the text: *Can the Ethiopian change his ſkin, or the leopard his ſpots? then may ye alſo do good who are accuſtomed to do evil.* Theſe words, we may obſerve, are not to be be strictly and literally understood, as if it were indeed as absolutely impossible for the sinner to correct and reform the disposition of his heart, as for the Ethiopian to change his skin. This illustration the prophet makes use of, only to mark the extreme difficulty **the sons** of wickedness may expect **to find, and** which approaches **near to a** natural impossibility to surmount, when they begin the work of reformation, at a time when their sins have acquired strength and maturity, and by long habits are deeply rooted in the mind.

In this discourse I shall consider, 1*st*, The danger of contracting, and the difficulty **of reforming, vitious** habits; and, 2*dly*, Shall observe, that though the task **be difficult, the difficulty may be overcome by proper resolution,** and the sinner may **have it in his** power **to** return to duty, and reconcile himself to God.

1. **There is in** human nature so unhappy an inclination and propensity to sin, that attention **and** vigilance are always requisite **to** oppose this inclination, and

maintain our integrity. Our paſſions and affections, inſtead of ſubmitting to the government of Reaſon, and acting under its directions, as was originally deſigned, are apt to remonſtrate againſt its orders, and diſclaim its authority. But when this innate propenſity to ſin, inſtead of being corrected and reformed by diſcipline and reaſon, acquires additional ſtrength by cuſtom and habit,—the difficulty of reſiſting, and the conſequent danger, become ſtill more inſurmountable. The power and influence of Habit is the ſubject of daily obſervation. Even in matters merely mechanical, where no attention of mind is required, cuſtom and practice give, we know, an expertneſs and facility not otherwiſe to be acquired. The caſe is the ſame, however unaccountable, in the operations of the mind. Actions frequently repeated, form habits; and habits approach near to natural propenſions. And ſuch is the nature of all habits, that the longer we perſevere, the more we are confirmed in them; and ſuch is our nature, that our actions

tions are more determined by custom and habit, than by principle.

But if such be the influence of habits in general, vitious ones are still more peculiarly powerful. If the power of custom be on all occasions apt to prevail, we shall have still less inclination to oppose it where the object to which we accustom ourselves is naturally agreeable and suited to our corruption. Here all the resolution we can summon to our assistance, will be requisite, and perhaps ineffectual. For if the first impulses of passion, the first assaults of temptation, are sometimes so hard to be resisted; what opposition can we make against them when they are aided and reinforced by habit and indulgence? How shall we be able, when we knew not how to sustain the first onset of vice; when yet shame and fear, when education and religion, were placed as guards upon our virtue;—how shall we be able to oppose the enemy, when those guards are removed, and we stand exposed to him defenceless and unarmed?

We may form an idea of the unhappy situation of an habitual offender, from the difficulty we find in conquering even an indifferent cuſtom. What was at firſt optional and voluntary, becomes by degrees in a manner neceſſary, and almoſt unavoidable. For although it is eaſy to contract ill habits, it is not without violence, and ſelf-denial, to which we are always averſe, that we can diſengage ourſelves from them, or even form a deſire to be diſengaged.

And yet, beſides the natural force of cuſtom and habit, other conſiderations there are, which add to the difficulty of reforming vitious manners. By vitious habits we impair the underſtanding, and our perception of the moral diſtinction of actions becomes leſs clear and diſtinct. The progreſs of iniquity is always gradual. No man becomes at once a proficient in wickedneſs; nor is it eaſy at firſt to diſregard the admonitions of reaſon and conſcience. Smaller offences, under the plauſible pretext of being ſuch, gain the firſt admit-

admittance to the heart: And he who has been induced to comply with one sin, because it is a small one, will be tempted to a second, from the consideration that it is not much worse: And the same plea will lead him on gradually to another, and another, of still greater magnitude. When he thus becomes familiar with sin, and suffers its frequent approaches, and finds that no harm has happened unto him, and that vengeance still suffers him to live,—he begins to think sin not so hateful in its nature, nor so fatal in its consequences, as it is represented: it assumes a less hideous shape; its deformity wears off; the horror **with** which it ought to be, and is at first generally attended, abates; he becomes reconciled to it; his judgment submits to his inclinations; every new sin is committed with less reluctance than the former; and he endeavours to find out reasons, such as they are, to justify and vindicate what he is determined to persist in, and to practise: And thus, by habits of sinning, we cloud the understanding, and render it in a manner incapable of diftinguifhing moral good and evil; and by degrees reduce ourfelves to that unhappy condition which the Apoftle defcribes by being *dead in trefpaffes and fins;* when all moral feeling, all fenfibility of virtue and religion, is fo far loft in us, that it is almoft as difficult to awake to a fenfe of duty and to newnefs of life, as it is to raife and reanimate the dead.

But further: As, by long practice and perfeverance in fin, we lofe or impair the moral difcernment and feeling of the mind; fo, by the fame means, we provoke the ALMIGHTY to withdraw his affifting Grace, long beftowed in vain. For though his Holy Spirit is always ready to lend fuccour to thofe who afk, and endeavour to co-operate with his influences; yet he will not, we are affured, ftrive with thofe who refift: but, being often oppofed and grieved, will at length retire, and abandon them to their own guidance, and to the counfels of their own corruption; no longer choofing thofe temples for his refidence,

dence, which they **have fo often,** and fo profanely, violated and defiled.

And how melancholy, how wretched, muft be the ftate of perfons thus forfaken by their GOD—left expofed to the affaults of temptations, and deftitute of that divine armour whereby **alone** they can be enabled to overcome **or** refift them! It **is not in** man, thus difordered **and depraved, to order his fteps aright.** The fervants and flaves of fin, we **cannot,** by our own unaffifted ftrength, refcue our**felves** from the fatal fervitude. For if, at the beft, we ftand in need of the **divine direction and** grace, how much more do we want the heavenly aid, when **our minds are totally** corrupt, when **we delight** in our bondage, are in love with our chains, and have not fo much as a defire of reftoration to liberty! For then, indeed, when we have moft occafion for fuch aid, we **have generally the** leaft inclination to apply for it. **For** when men begin to have a difcernment of the fatal error and confequences of their conduct,—ftruck with a sense of their danger, they are apt to despair of that grace which they have so oft received in vain. Conscious of guilt, they are afraid to look up to that God whom they have so much offended. Self-convicted, they cannot lift up their eyes to Heaven with any hopes of mercy and forgiveness there. For all these reasons, it is dangerous to contract, difficult to reform, vitious habits.

II. Yet, notwithstanding this difficulty and danger, the sinner may have it in his power to return to duty, and reconcile himself to God. The occasion of despondency in this situation, is the remorse men feel from a consciousness of guilt; which yet is a favourable symptom, as it indicates a disposition and desire to recover themselves from it. Though the sinner, when he scrutinises his conduct, may find in it all the grounds and reasons of despair; yet due consideration of the patience, the compassion, and goodness of God, may, in the most desponding mind, kindle hopes of mercy. When once the sinner

sinner feels his guilt,—feels just impressions of his own disobedience, and of the consequent displeasure and resentment of Heaven; if he is serious in his resolutions to restore himself by repentance to the favour of his offended God; God, who is ever ready to meet and receive the returning penitent, will assist his resolution with such a portion of his grace, as may be sufficient, if not totally, at once, to extirpate vitious habits (for such sudden, instantaneous conversions we are not to expect), yet gradually to produce a disposition to virtue; so that, if not wanting to himself, he shall not fail to become superior to the power of inveterate habits. In this case, indeed, no endeavours on his part ought to be neglected,—no attempts left unessayed, to recommend himself to the throne of mercy.

From what has been observed, they who are young, and as yet unpractised in the vices of the world, may learn, wisely to consider with what facility and advantage they may now enter upon the duties of religion,

gion, whilst the mind is disengaged—not enslaved by vitious habits, free from bad impressions, and capable of the best. Whereas, if they neglect this opportunity of giving virtue prior possession of the heart, and of forming their manners by its rules, and should unhappily suffer sin and vice to get admittance there,—these will be every day extending their influence, and acquiring additional strength; and it will be a work of difficulty and labour to conquer and expel them.

Never, therefore, think of postponing the care of your salvation to the day of old age; never think of treasuring up to yourselves difficulties, sorrows, repentance, and remorse, against an age, the disorders and infirmities of which are themselves so hard to be sustained. Let not these be the comforts reserved for that period of life which stands most in need of consolation. What confusion must cover the self-convicted sinner, grown old in iniquity! How must he wish to blot out the memory of former years, when he looks back and

and sees them marked with various guilt, and filled up with a succession of vices and crimes! And how will he be able, when bending beneath the burden of years and infirmities, to attempt the conquest of habits by which he has been always enslaved,—and to disengage himself from chains in which he has long been a captive! How reluctant to attempt a task to which he has always been unequal; and to travel a difficult road, which opens to him, indeed, happier prospects, but has hitherto been found impracticable! Remember, therefore, your CREATOR in the days of your youth.

But if any of us have unhappily lost this first, best season of devoting ourselves to GOD,—and have reserved nothing but shame, sorrow, and remorse, for the entertainment of riper years;—let the review of former transgressions be an incitement to immediate repentance; let us, without delay, apply our heart to the work of salvation, with an attention suited to its importance, and with a resolution equal to the difficulties occasioned by the influence of long established habits:—and then we have good grounds to hope that the necessary aids of Divine Grace will not be wanting; that we may look up to Heaven with hopes of mercy; that, however we may be tied and bound with the chain of our sins, our MAKER will stretch forth the right hand of his power to save and deliver us. For the GOD of truth hath assured us, that he will give his Holy Spirit to them that ask it: that no time is limited when the gate of mercy shall be shut against the penitent: that *whenever the wicked man will turn from his sins that he hath committed, and do that which is lawful and right, all his transgressions that he hath committed, shall not be mentioned unto him; in his righteousness that he hath done he shall live.*

F I N I S.

www.ingramcontent.com/pod-product-compliance
Lightning Source LLC
Chambersburg PA
CBHW030424300426
44112CB00009B/848